PRO FOOTBALL RECORDS

A GUIDE FOR EVERY FAN

BY SHANE FREDERICK

COMPASS POINT BOOKS
a capstone imprint

Compass Point Books are published by Capstone
1710 Roe Crest Drive, North Mankato, Minnesota 56003
www.mycapstone.com

Editorial Credits
Lauren Dupuis-Perez, editor; Sara Radka, designer; Eric Gohl, media researcher;
Laura Manthe, production specialist

Library of Congress Cataloging-in-Publication Data
Library of Congress Cataloging-in-Publication data is available on the Library of
Congress website.

ISBN 978-1-5435-5461-8 (library binding)
ISBN 978-1-5435-5933-0 (paperback)
ISBN 978-1-5435-5466-3 (eBook PDF)

Photo Credits
Getty Images: Allsport/Jon Ferrey, 27, Donald Miralle, 10 (top), 49 (bottom), George
Rose, 30 (bottom), Gregory Shamus, 7 (bottom), Harry How, 13 (top), iStockphoto/
Nastco, background, Jamie Squire, 10 (bottom), Jason Hanna, 14 (top), Maddie
Meyer, 11 (bottom), Mark Konezny, 7 (top), NFLPhotoLibrary/Robert B. Stanton,
15, Otto Greule Jr, 50, Stephen Dunn, 4, 11 (top), Wesley Hitt, 56; Newscom: Ai
Wire/Vern Verna, 54, Ai Wire/Yelman, 8 (bottom), Cal Sport Media/Duncan
Williams, 33 (top), 39, Everett Collection/CSU Archives, 8 (top), Icon SMI/Cliff
Welch, 29 (bottom), Icon SMI/John W. McDonough, 46, Icon SMI/Ric Tapia, 21
(top), Icon SMI/Thomas B. Shea, 61 (bottom), Icon Sportswire/Al Golub, 31, Icon
Sportswire/Aric Becker, 22 (bottom), Icon Sportswire/Cliff Welch, 32 (bottom),
Icon Sportswire/John Cordes, 32 (top), 42 (bottom), Icon Sportswire/Roy K. Miller,
38, Icon Sportswire/Samuel Stringer, 23 (bottom), Icon Sportswire/Scott Grau, 37,
Icon Sportswire/Zach Bolinger, 20 (top), Image of Sport, 25, KRT, 14 (bottom), 17,
22 (top), 55, 57, KRT/Eliot J. Schechter, 35 (top), MCT/Colorado Springs Gazette/
Christian Murdock, 49 (top), MCT/Minneapolis Star Tribune/Elizabeth Flores,
29 (top), MCT/Sun Sentinel/Jim Rassol, 19, Richard Marshall, 21 (bottom), Rob
Tringali, 51, Ron Wyatt, 43 (top), 59 (bottom), SCG/Frank Jansky, 58 (left), Sipa
USA/Anthony Behar, 44, Sipa USA/David Clements, 45 (bottom), SplashNews/
Charlie Ans, 36, UPI/Andy Newman, 9, UPI/Kevin Dietsch, 47, UPI/Terry Smith,
6, ZUMA Wire/Amy Sanderson, 58 (bottom right), ZUMA Wire/CNP/Ron Sachs,
48, ZUMA Wire/Contra Costa Times/Bob Larson, 34 (top), ZUMA Wire/Contra
Costa Times/Karl Mondon, 16 (top), ZUMA Wire/Dan Anderson, 40, ZUMA Wire/
Globe Photos/John Barrett, 45 (top), ZUMA Wire/Minneapolis Star Tribune/Carlos
Gonzalez, 35 (bottom), ZUMA Wire/NewSport/Steve Boyle, 33 (bottom), ZUMA
Wire/Scott A. Miller, 16 (bottom), 18, 23 (top), 24, 30 (top), 34 (bottom), 42 (top),
43 (bottom), 58 (top right), 59 (top), 60; Shutterstock: David Lee, cover (football),
wavebreakmedia, cover (foot); Wikimedia: KIIS Radio/Los Angeles Rams/Los
Angeles County Sheriff's Department, 13 (bottom), packers.com, 61 (top), U.S. Air
Force photo/Staff Sgt. Henry Hoegen, 12, Underwood & Underwood, 20 (bottom)

All stats are through the 2017 NFL regular season and following postseason.

Printed in the United States of America.
PA49

Table of Contents

CHAPTER 1

Player Records......6

CHAPTER 2

Team Records......36

CHAPTER 3

Postseason Records......40

CHAPTER 4

Around the Field......56

Read More 62

Internet Sites 62

Index 62

RECORDS OF
THE GRIDIRON

In 2004, Peyton Manning broke a National Football League (NFL) record that had stood for 20 seasons. The Indianapolis Colts quarterback threw his 49th touchdown pass that season. This surpassed the standard of 48 set by Dolphins great Dan Marino.

Manning's record didn't last two decades like Marino's did, however. Just three seasons later, the Patriots' Tom Brady did one better. He tossed 50 touchdown passes while leading his team's almost unstoppable offense. Not to be outdone, Manning returned to the top of the list in 2013. This time, he was the quarterback of the high-flying Denver Broncos. He finished that season with 55 scoring strikes!

In the pass-happy NFL, it wouldn't be surprising to see Manning's record beaten again someday soon. Who will do it, though? A veteran such as the Packers' Aaron Rodgers or the Seahawks' Russell Wilson? What about an up-and-comer such as the Eagles' Carson Wentz or the Rams' Jared Goff?

What do you think is the greatest record in NFL history? Is it Manning's touchdown total? Maybe it's Brett Favre's starting streak, Emmitt Smith's career rushing yards, or the Broncos' 2013 point total. Not sure? Read on—you're bound to find your favorite!

RECORD FACT

Records for pro football have been kept since 1920. Back then, the National Football League was known as the American Professional Football Association. Two years later, its name was changed. It is now known as the NFL.

CHAPTER 1

Player Records

If you read through the NFL's individual records, one name seems to appear more than any other: Jerry Rice. The wide receiver played most of his career with the 49ers. He ranks among the leaders on several offensive statistics and sits at the top of some of the greatest lists in football history. He holds career records for total touchdowns, touchdown receptions, catches, receiving yards, and all-purpose yards. And those are just regular-season records!

Records can be set over the course of an entire career, a season, or a single game or play. Setting a record is a historic event. It establishes a player as one of the greats of the sport. That player sets a bar that veteran players aim to reach before they retire. It's also a goal that young and future players dream about achieving.

Few players could catch Jerry Rice on the football field. Even fewer have caught him in the record books. But even making it into the top 10 of an individual statistical category is considered a great accomplishment.

Passing Touchdowns

CAREER

1	Peyton Manning	539	Colts/Broncos	1998–2015
2	Brett Favre	508	Falcons/Packers/Jets/Vikings	1991–2010
3	Tom Brady	488	Patriots	2000–2017*
	Drew Brees	488	Chargers/Saints	2001–2017*
5	Dan Marino	420	Dolphins	1983–1999
6	Fran Tarkenton	342	Vikings/Giants	1961–1978
	Philip Rivers	342	Chargers	2004–2017*
8	Eli Manning	339	Giants	2004–2017*
9	Ben Roethlisberger	329	Steelers	2004–2017*
10	Aaron Rodgers	313	Packers	2005–2017*

* active player

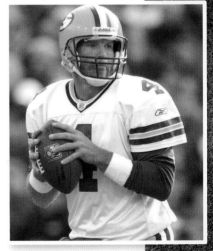

▲ **Brett Favre**

SINGLE SEASON

1	Peyton Manning	55	Broncos	2013
2	Tom Brady	50	Patriots	2007
3	Peyton Manning	49	Colts	2004
4	Dan Marino	48	Dolphins	1984
5	Drew Brees	46	Saints	2011
6	Aaron Rodgers	45	Packers	2011
7	Dan Marino	44	Dolphins	1986
8	Drew Brees	43	Saints	2012
9	Kurt Warner	41	Rams	1999
	Matthew Stafford	41	Lions	2011

▲ **Tom Brady**

Passing Touchdowns

SINGLE GAME

Eight quarterbacks in NFL history have thrown seven touchdown passes in a single game. Most recent was the Saints' Drew Brees. Brees did it on November 1, 2015, against the Giants. Here are the others:

Nick Foles	Eagles	Nov. 3, 2013
Peyton Manning	Broncos	Sept. 5, 2013
Joe Kapp	Vikings	Sept. 28, 1969
Y.A. Tittle	Giants	Oct. 28, 1962
George Blanda	Oilers	Nov. 19, 1961
Adrian Burk	Eagles	Oct. 17, 1954
Sid Luckman	Bears	Nov. 14, 1943

▲ Sid Luckman

Passing Yards

CAREER

1	**Peyton Manning**	71,940	Colts/Broncos	1998–2015
2	**Brett Favre**	71,838	Falcons/Packers/Jets/Vikings	1991–2010
3	**Drew Brees**	70,445	Chargers/Saints	2001–2017*
4	**Tom Brady**	66,159	Patriots	2000–2017*
5	**Dan Marino**	61,361	Dolphins	1983–1999
6	**Eli Manning**	51,682	Giants	2004–2017*
7	**John Elway**	51,475	Broncos	1983–1998
8	**Ben Roethlisberger**	51,065	Steelers	2004–2017*
9	**Philip Rivers**	50,348	Chargers	2004–2017*
10	**Warren Moon**	49,325	Oilers/Vikings/Seahawks/Chiefs	1984–2000

active player

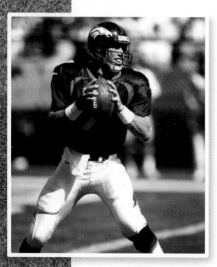

▲ John Elway

Passing Yards

SINGLE SEASON

1	**Peyton Manning**	5,477	Broncos	2013
2	**Drew Brees**	5,476	Saints	2011
3	**Tom Brady**	5,235	Patriots	2011
4	**Drew Brees**	5,208	Saints	2016
5	**Drew Brees**	5,177	Saints	2012
6	**Drew Brees**	5,162	Saints	2013
7	**Dan Marino**	5,084	Dolphins	1984
8	**Drew Brees**	5,069	Saints	2008
9	**Matthew Stafford**	5,038	Lions	2011
10	**Matthew Stafford**	4,967	Lions	2012

▲ Dan Marino

SINGLE GAME

1	**Norm Van Brocklin**	554	Rams	Sept. 28, 1951
2	**Warren Moon**	527	Oilers	Dec. 16, 1990
	Matt Schaub	527	Texans	Nov. 18, 2012
4	**Boomer Esiason**	522	Cardinals	Nov. 10, 1996
	Ben Roethlisberger	522	Steelers	Oct. 26, 2014
6	**Dan Marino**	521	Dolphins	Oct. 23, 1998
7	**Matthew Stafford**	520	Lions	Jan. 1, 2012
8	**Tom Brady**	517	Patriots	Sept. 12, 2011
9	**Phil Simms**	513	Giants	Oct. 13, 1985
	Derek Carr	513	Raiders	Oct. 30, 2016

RECORD FACT

Before he played in the NFL, Warren Moon spent six seasons in the Canadian Football League. He helped the Edmonton Eskimos win five straight Grey Cup championships. During his CFL career, he compiled 21,228 passing yards and 144 touchdown passes. Add those to his NFL numbers and he'd rank third in passing yards and 5th in touchdown passes.

Completions

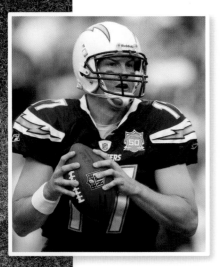

▲ Philip Rivers

CAREER

1	**Brett Favre**	6,300	Falcons/Packers/Jets/Vikings	1991–2010
2	**Drew Brees**	6,222	Chargers/Saints	2001–2017*
3	**Peyton Manning**	6,125	Colts/Broncos	1998–2015
4	**Tom Brady**	5,629	Patriots	2000–2017*
5	**Dan Marino**	4,967	Dolphins	1983–1999
6	**Eli Manning**	4,424	Giants	2004–2017*
7	**Philip Rivers**	4,171	Chargers	2004–2017*
8	**Ben Roethlisberger**	4,164	Steelers	2004–2017*
9	**John Elway**	4,123	Broncos	1983–1998
10	**Warren Moon**	3,988	Oilers/Vikings/Seahawks/Chiefs	1984–2000

* active player

▲ Drew Brees

SINGLE SEASON

1	**Drew Brees**	471	Saints	2016
2	**Drew Brees**	468	Saints	2011
3	**Drew Brees**	456	Saints	2014
4	**Peyton Manning**	450	Colts	2010
	Peyton Manning	450	Broncos	2013
6	**Drew Brees**	448	Saints	2010
7	**Drew Brees**	446	Saints	2013
8	**Drew Brees**	440	Saints	2007
9	**Matt Ryan**	439	Falcons	2013
10	**Philip Rivers**	437	Chargers	2015

SINGLE GAME

1	**Drew Bledsoe**	45	Patriots	Nov. 13, 1994
2	**Ben Roethlisberger**	44	Steelers	Dec. 10, 2017
3	**Rich Gannon**	43	Raiders	Sept. 15, 2002
	Matt Schaub	43	Texans	Nov. 18, 2012
	Philip Rivers	43	Chargers	Oct. 18, 2015
	Tom Brady	43	Patriots	Feb. 5, 2017
7	**Vinny Testaverde**	42	Jets	Dec. 6, 1998
	Richard Todd	42	Jets	Sept. 21, 1980
9	**Warren Moon**	41	Oilers	Nov. 10, 1991
	Tony Romo	41	Cowboys	Dec. 6, 2009
	Eli Manning	41	Giants	Oct. 11, 2015
	Kirk Cousins	41	Redskins	Nov. 24, 2016

▲ Rich Gannon

RATING THE QUARTERBACK

A complex formula is used to determine how well a quarterback is playing. It's called "passer rating." It takes into account the following factors: completions, attempts, passing yards, touchdown passes, and interceptions. In 2011, the Packers' Aaron Rodgers set the single-season passer rating record, scoring 122.5 (158.3 would be a perfect record). Rodgers also holds the career mark, at 103.8. He's the only QB with a career rating of more than 100.

Interceptions

▲ Vinny
Testaverde

CAREER

1	**Brett Favre**	336	Falcons/Packers/Jets/Vikings	1991–2010
2	**George Blanda**	277	Bears/Colts/Oilers/Raiders	1949–1975
3	**John Hadl**	268	Chargers/Rams/Packers/Oilers	1962–1977
4	**Vinny Testaverde**	267	Buccaneers/Browns/Ravens/Jets/Cowboys/Patriots/Panthers	1987–2007
5	**Fran Tarkenton**	266	Vikings/Giants	1961–1978
6	**Norm Snead**	257	Redskins/Eagles/Vikings/Giants/49ers	1961–1976
7	**Johnny Unitas**	253	Colts/Chargers	1956–1973
8	**Dan Marino**	252	Dolphins	1983–1999
9	**Peyton Manning**	251	Colts/Broncos	1998–2015
10	**Y.A. Tittle**	248	Colts/49ers/Giants	1948–1964

SINGLE SEASON

1	**George Blanda**	42	Oilers	1962
2	**Vinny Testaverde**	35	Buccaneers	1998
3	**Frank Tripucka**	34	Broncos	1960
4	**Fran Tarkenton**	32	Vikings	1978
	John Hadl	32	Chargers	1968
6	**Sid Luckman**	31	Bears	1947
7	**Al Dorow**	30	Titans (NY)	1961
	George Blanda	30	Oilers	1965
	Jim Hart	30	Cardinals	1967
	Ken Stabler	30	Raiders	1978
	Richard Todd	30	Jets	1980

RECORD FACT

Quarterback Jim Hardy of the Chicago Cardinals has the dubious distinction of throwing eight interceptions in a single game. It happened in a game against the Eagles in 1950. It's a record that may never be broken. Six players have thrown seven picks in a game, most recently Ty Detmer of the Lions in 2001.

RUSHING

Rushing Yards

CAREER

1	**Emmitt Smith**	18,355	Cowboys/Cardinals	1990–2004
2	**Walter Payton**	16,726	Bears	1975–1987
3	**Barry Sanders**	15,269	Lions	1989–1998
4	**Curtis Martin**	14,101	Patriots/Jets	1995–2005
5	**Frank Gore**	14,026	49ers/Colts	2005–2017*
6	**LaDainian Tomlinson**	13,684	Chargers/Jets	2001–2011
7	**Jerome Bettis**	13,662	Rams/Steelers	1993–2005
8	**Eric Dickerson**	13,259	Rams/Colts/Raiders/Falcons	1983–1993
9	**Tony Dorsett**	12,739	Cowboys/Broncos	1977–1988
10	**Jim Brown**	12,312	Browns	1957–1965

active player

▲ Curtis Martin

SINGLE SEASON

1	**Eric Dickerson**	2,105	Rams	1984
2	**Adrian Peterson**	2,097	Vikings	2012
3	**Jamal Lewis**	2,066	Ravens	2003
4	**Barry Sanders**	2,053	Lions	1997
5	**Terrell Davis**	2,008	Broncos	1998
6	**Chris Johnson**	2,006	Titans	2009
7	**O.J. Simpson**	2,003	Bills	1973
8	**Earl Campbell**	1,934	Oilers	1980
9	**Barry Sanders**	1,883	Lions	1994
	Ahman Green	1,883	Packers	2003

▲ Eric Dickerson

Rushing Yards

SINGLE GAME

1	**Adrian Peterson**	296	Vikings	Nov. 4, 2007
2	**Jamal Lewis**	295	Ravens	Sept. 14, 2003
3	**Jerome Harrison**	286	Browns	Dec. 20, 2009
4	**Corey Dillon**	278	Bengals	Oct. 22, 2000
5	**Walter Payton**	275	Bears	Nov. 20, 1977
6	**O.J. Simpson**	273	Bills	Nov. 25, 1976
7	**Shaun Alexander**	266	Seahawks	Nov. 11, 2001
8	**Jamaal Charles**	259	Chiefs	Jan. 3, 2010
9	**DeMarco Murray**	253	Cowboys	Oct. 23, 2011
10	**Mike Anderson**	251	Broncos	Dec. 3, 2000
	Doug Martin	251	Buccaneers	Nov. 4, 2012

▲ Jamaal Charles

Rushing Touchdowns

CAREER

1	**Emmitt Smith**	164	Cowboys/Cardinals	1990–2004
2	**LaDainian Tomlinson**	145	Chargers/Jets	2001–2011
3	**Marcus Allen**	123	Raiders/Chiefs	1982–1997
4	**Walter Payton**	110	Bears	1975–1987
5	**Jim Brown**	106	Browns	1957–1965
6	**John Riggins**	104	Jets/Redskins	1971–1985
7	**Shaun Alexander**	100	Seahawks/Redskins	2000–2008
	Marshall Faulk	100	Colts/Rams	1994–2005
9	**Barry Sanders**	99	Lions	1989–1998
	Adrian Peterson	99	Vikings/Saints/Cardinals	2007–2017*

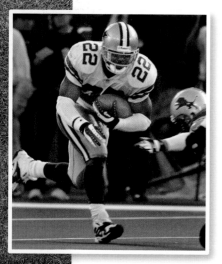

▲ Emmitt Smith

active player

SINGLE SEASON

1	LaDainian Tomlinson	28	Chargers	2006
2	Priest Holmes	27	Chiefs	2003
	Shaun Alexander	27	Seahawks	2005
4	Emmitt Smith	25	Cowboys	1995
5	John Riggins	24	Redskins	1983
6	Joe Morris	21	Giants	1985
	Emmitt Smith	21	Cowboys	1994
	Terry Allen	21	Redskins	1996
	Terrell Davis	21	Broncos	1998
	Priest Holmes	21	Chiefs	2002

▲ LaDainian Tomlinson

LONGEST RUN

1	Tony Dorsett	99	Cowboys	Jan. 3, 1983
2	Ahman Green	98	Packers	Dec. 28, 2003
3	Andy Uram	97	Packers	Oct. 8, 1939
	Bob Gage	97	Steelers	Dec. 4, 1949
	Lamar Miller	97	Dolphins	Dec. 28, 2014
6	Jim Spavital	96	Colts	Nov. 5, 1950
	Bob Hoernschemeyer	96	Lions	Nov. 23, 1950
	Garrison Hearst	96	49ers	Sept. 6, 1998
	Corey Dillon	96	Bengals	Oct. 28, 2001
10	Chester Taylor	95	Vikings	Oct. 22, 2006
	Tiki Barber	95	Giants	Dec. 31, 2005

RECORD FACT

Quarterbacks are known for throwing touchdown passes, but the Panthers' Cam Newton is a true dual threat. He holds the record for rushing TDs by a quarterback, with 54 as of the 2017 season.

Receptions

▲ Jerry Rice

CAREER

1	Jerry Rice	1,549	49ers/Raiders/Seahawks	1985–2004
2	Tony Gonzalez	1,325	Chiefs/Falcons	1997–2013
3	Larry Fitzgerald	1,234	Cardinals	2004–2017*
4	Jason Witten	1,152	Cowboys	2003–2017
5	Marvin Harrison	1,102	Colts	1996–2008
6	Cris Carter	1,101	Eagles/Vikings/Dolphins	1987–2002
7	Tim Brown	1,094	Raiders/Buccaneers	1988–2004
8	Terrell Owens	1,078	49ers/Eagles/Cowboys/Bills/Bengals	1996–2010
9	Anquan Boldin	1076	Cardinals/Ravens/49ers/Lions	2003–2016
10	Reggie Wayne	1,070	Colts	2001–2014

* active player

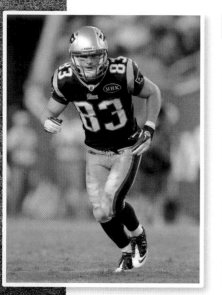

▲ Wes Welker

SINGLE SEASON

1	Marvin Harrison	143	Colts	2002
2	Antonio Brown	136	Steelers	2015
	Julio Jones	136	Falcons	2015
4	Antonio Brown	129	Steelers	2014
5	Herman Moore	123	Lions	1995
	Wes Welker	123	Patriots	2009
7	Cris Carter	122	Vikings	1994
	Cris Carter	122	Vikings	1995
	Jerry Rice	122	49ers	1995
	Wes Welker	122	Patriots	2011
	Calvin Johnson	122	Lions	2012

1	Brandon Marshall	21	Broncos	Dec. 13, 2009
2	Terrell Owens	20	49ers	Dec. 17, 2000
3	Tom Fears	18	Rams	Dec. 3, 1950
	Brandon Marshall	18	Broncos	Sept. 14, 2008
	Jason Witten	18	Cowboys	Oct. 28, 2012
6	Clark Gaines	17	Jets	Sept. 21, 1980
	Antonio Brown	17	Steelers	Nov. 8, 2015
8	Sonny Randle	16	Cardinals	Nov. 4, 1962
	Jerry Rice	16	49ers	Nov. 20, 1994
	Keenan McCardell	16	Jaguars	Oct. 20, 1996
	Troy Brown	16	Patriots	Sept. 22, 2002
	Wes Welker	16	Patriots	Sept. 25, 2011
	Antonio Brown	16	Steelers	Dec. 20, 2015

▲ Terrell Owens

Receiving Yards

CAREER

1	Jerry Rice	22,895	49ers/Raiders/Seahawks	1985–2004
2	Terrell Owens	15,934	49ers/Eagles/Cowboys/Bills/Bengals	1996–2010
3	Larry Fitzgerald	15,545	Cardinals	2004–2017*
4	Randy Moss	15,292	Vikings/Raiders/Patriots/Titans/49ers	1998–2012
5	Isaac Bruce	15,208	Rams/49ers	1994–2009
6	Tony Gonzalez	15,127	Chiefs/Falcons	1997–2013
7	Tim Brown	14,934	Raiders/Buccaneers	1988–2004
8	Steve Smith	14,731	Panthers/Ravens	2001–2016
9	Marvin Harrison	14,580	Colts	1996–2008
10	Reggie Wayne	14,345	Colts	2001–2014

active player

RECORD FACT

In 2017, Chargers receiver Keenan Allen became the first player in NFL history to make at least 90 catches and also haul in an interception on defense in a single season. He finished the season with 102 receptions.

Receiving yards

▲ Calvin Johnson

SINGLE SEASON

1	Calvin Johnson	1,964	Lions	2012
2	Julio Jones	1,871	Falcons	2015
3	Jerry Rice	1,848	49ers	1995
4	Antonio Brown	1,834	Steelers	2015
5	Isaac Bruce	1,781	Rams	1995
6	Charley Hennigan	1,746	Oilers	1961
7	Marvin Harrison	1,722	Colts	2002
8	Antonio Brown	1,698	Steelers	2014
9	Torry Holt	1,696	Rams	2003
10	Herman Moore	1,686	Lions	1995

SINGLE GAME

1	Flipper Anderson	336	Rams	Nov. 26, 1989
2	Calvin Johnson	329	Lions	Oct. 27, 2013
3	Stephone Paige	309	Chiefs	Dec. 22, 1985
4	Jim Benton	303	Rams	Nov. 22, 1945
5	Cloyce Box	302	Lions	Dec. 3, 1950
6	Julio Jones	300	Falcons	Oct. 2, 2016
7	Jimmy Smith	291	Jaguars	Sept. 10, 2000
8	Jerry Rice	289	49ers	Dec. 18, 1995
9	John Taylor	286	49ers	Dec. 11, 1989
10	Antonio Brown	284	Steelers	Nov. 8, 2015

RECORD FACT

There have been 13 pass plays for 99 yards in NFL history, all touchdowns. Wes Welker of the Patriots and Victor Cruz of the Giants hauled in those long passes during the 2011 season. In 1972, Ahmad Rashad (then known as Bobby Moore) was involved in the longest pass play that didn't result in a score. The 98-yard play started at the Cardinals' 1-yard line and ended when Moore was tackled at the opposite 1-yard line.

Receiving Touchdowns

CAREER

1	**Jerry Rice**	197	49ers/Raiders/Seahawks	1985–2004
2	**Randy Moss**	156	Vikings/Raiders/Patriots/Titans/49ers	1998–2012
3	**Terrell Owens**	153	49ers/Eagles/Cowboys/Bills/Bengals	1996–2010
4	**Cris Carter**	130	Eagles/Vikings/Dolphins	1987–2002
5	**Marvin Harrison**	128	Colts	1996–2008
6	**Antonio Gates**	114	Chargers	2003–2017*
7	**Tony Gonzalez**	111	Chiefs/Falcons	1997–2013
8	**Larry Fitzgerald**	110	Cardinals	2004–2017*
9	**Steve Largent**	100	Seahawks	1976–1989
	Tim Brown	100	Raiders/Buccaneers	1988–2004

* active player

RECORD FACT

Three players in NFL history have caught five touchdown passes in a single game: the 49ers' Jerry Rice (1990), the Chargers' Kellen Winslow (1981), and the Cardinals' Bob Shaw (1950).

SINGLE SEASON

1	**Randy Moss**	23	Patriots	2007
2	**Jerry Rice**	22	49ers	1987
3	**Mark Clayton**	18	Dolphins	1984
	Sterling Sharpe	18	Packers	1994
5	**Don Hutson**	17	Packers	1942
	Elroy Hirsch	17	Rams	1951
	Bill Groman	17	Oilers	1961
	Jerry Rice	17	49ers	1989
	Carl Pickens	17	Bengals	1995
	Cris Carter	17	Vikings	1995
	Randy Moss	17	Vikings	1998
	Randy Moss	17	Vikings	2003
	Rob Gronkowski	17	Patriots	2011

▲ Randy Moss

Points

CAREER

1	**Morten Andersen**	K	2,544	Saints/Falcons/Giants/Chiefs/Vikings	1982–2007
2	**Adam Vinatieri**	K	2,487	Patriots/Colts	1996–2017*
3	**Gary Anderson**	K	2,434	Steelers/Eagles/49ers/Vikings/Titans	1982–2004
4	**Jason Hanson**	K	2,150	Lions	1992–2012
5	**John Carney**	K	2,062	Buccaneers/Chargers/Rams/Saints/Chiefs/Jaguars/Giants	1988–2010
6	**Matt Stover**	K	2,004	Browns/Ravens/Colts	1991–2009
7	**George Blanda**	QB/K	2,002	Colts/Bears/Oilers/Raiders	1949–1975
8	**Jason Elam**	K	1,983	Broncos/Falcons	1993–2009
9	**John Kasay**	K	1,970	Seahawks/Panthers/Saints	1991–2011
10	**Phil Dawson**	K	1,817	Browns/49ers/Cardinals	1999–2017*

* active player

▲ Adam Vinatieri

POINT PRODUCERS

The Cardinals' Ernie Nevers, the Browns' Dub Jones, and the Bears' Gale Sayers are the only players to score six touchdowns in one game. Nevers holds the NFL record for points in a game with 40 (six rushing TDs and four extra-point kicks in 1929). Jones and Sayers each had 36 points. The Packers' Paul Hornung once scored 33 points in a game.

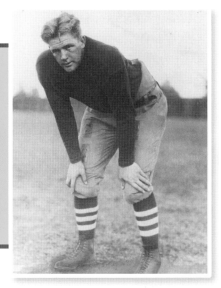

▲ Ernie Nevers

SINGLE SEASON

1	LaDainian Tomlinson	RB	186	Chargers	2006
2	Paul Hornung	RB/K	176	Packers	1960
3	Shaun Alexander	RB	168	Seahawks	2005
4	David Akers	K	166	49ers	2011
5	Gary Anderson	K	164	Vikings	1998
6	Jeff Wilkins	K	163	Rams	2003
7	Priest Holmes	RB	162	Chiefs	2003
8	Mark Moseley	K	161	Redskins	1983
9	Marshall Faulk	RB	160	Rams	2000
10	Stephen Gostkowski	K	158	Patriots	2013
	Matt Bryant	K	158	Falcons	2016
	Greg Zuerlein	K	158	Rams	2017

▲ David Akers

Touchdowns

CAREER

1	Jerry Rice	WR	208	49ers/Raiders/Seahawks	1985–2004
2	Emmitt Smith	RB	175	Cowboys/Cardinals	1990–2004
3	LaDainian Tomlinson	RB	162	Chargers/Jets	2001–2011
4	Randy Moss	WR	157	Vikings/Raiders/Patriots/Titans/49ers	1998–2012
5	Terrell Owens	WR	156	49ers/Eagles/Cowboys/Bills/Bengals	1996–2010
6	Marcus Allen	RB	145	Raiders/Chiefs	1982–1997
7	Marshall Faulk	RB	136	Colts/Rams	1994–2005
8	Cris Carter	WR	131	Eagles/Vikings/Dolphins	1987–2002
9	Marvin Harrison	WR	128	Colts	1996–2008
10	Jim Brown	RB	126	Browns	1957–1965

▲ Cris Carter

Touchdowns

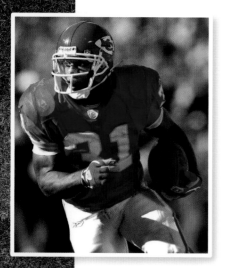

▲ Priest Holmes

SINGLE SEASON

1	LaDainian Tomlinson	RB	31	Chargers	2006
2	Shaun Alexander	RB	28	Seahawks	2005
3	Priest Holmes	RB	27	Chiefs	2003
4	Marshall Faulk	RB	26	Rams	2000
5	Emmitt Smith	RB	25	Cowboys	1995
6	John Riggins	RB	24	Redskins	1983
	Priest Holmes	RB	24	Chiefs	2002
8	O.J. Simpson	RB	23	Bills	1975
	Jerry Rice	WR	23	49ers	1987
	Terrell Davis	RB	23	Broncos	1998
	Randy Moss	WR	23	Patriots	2007

DEFENSIVE SCORERS

Three players in NFL history are tied for the most defensive touchdowns. They have each scored 13 times on interception and fumble returns in regular-season games. They are Charles Woodson, Rod Woodson, and Darren Sharper, all defensive backs.

▶ Charles Woodson

KICKING

Field Goals

CAREER

1	Morten Andersen	565	Saints/Falcons/Giants/Chiefs/Vikings	1982–2007
2	Adam Vinatieri	559	Patriots/Colts	1996–2017*
3	Gary Anderson	538	Steelers/Eagles/49ers/Vikings/Titans	1982–2004
4	Jason Hanson	495	Lions	1992–2012
5	John Carney	478	Buccaneers/Chargers/Rams/Saints/Chiefs/Jaguars/Giants	1988–2010
6	Matt Stover	471	Browns/Ravens/Colts	1991–2009
7	John Kasay	461	Seahawks/Panthers/Saints	1991–2011
8	Jason Elam	436	Broncos/Falcons	1993–2009
	Phil Dawson	436	Browns/49ers/Cardinals	1999–2017*
10	Sebastian Janikowski	414	Raiders	2000–2016

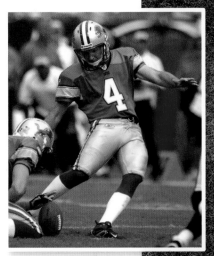

▲ Jason Hanson

* active player

SINGLE SEASON

1	David Akers	44	49ers	2011
2	Neil Rackers	40	Cardinals	2005
3	Robbie Gould	39	49ers	2017
	Olindo Mare	39	Dolphins	1999
	Jeff Wilkins	39	Rams	2003
6	Stephen Gostkowski	38	Patriots	2013
	Justin Tucker	38	Ravens	2013
	Justin Tucker	38	Ravens	2016
	Greg Zuerlein	38	Rams	2017
	Harrison Butker	38	Chiefs	2017

▲ Robbie Gould

Field Goals

SINGLE GAME

1	**Rob Bironas**	8	Titans	Oct. 21, 2007
2	**Jim Bakken**	7	Cardinals	Sept. 24, 1967
	Rich Karlis	7	Vikings	Nov. 5, 1989
	Chris Boniol	7	Cowboys	Nov. 18, 1996
	Billy Cundiff	7	Cowboys	Sept. 15, 2003
	Shayne Graham	7	Bengals	Nov. 11, 2007
	Cairo Santos	7	Chiefs	Oct. 4, 2015
	Greg Zuerlein	7	Rams	Oct. 1, 2017

LEGGING IT OUT

On November 8, 1970, the Saints' Tom Dempsey kicked a 63-yard field goal, setting an NFL record. The feat was matched three times—by the Broncos' Jason Elam (1998), the Raiders' Sebastian Janikowski (2011), and the 49ers' David Akers (2012). Finally, on December 8, 2013, the long-standing record was broken. Matt Prater nailed a 64-yarder for the Broncos in a game against the Titans in the thin air of Denver, Colorado. Janikowski has the record for the longest field goal attempt, coming up short on a try of 76 yards.

Interceptions

CAREER

1	**Paul Krause**	81	Redskins/Vikings	1964–1979
2	**Emlen Tunnell**	79	Giants/Packers	1948–1961
3	**Rod Woodson**	71	Steelers/49ers/Ravens/Raiders	1987–2003
4	**Dick Lane**	68	Rams/Cardinals/Lions	1952–1965
5	**Ken Riley**	65	Bengals	1969–1983
	Charles Woodson	65	Raiders/Packers	1998–2015
7	**Ed Reed**	64	Ravens/Texans/Jets	2002–2013
8	**Ronnie Lott**	63	49ers/Raiders/Jets	1981–1994
	Darren Sharper	63	Packers/Vikings/Saints	1997–2010

▲ Rod Woodson

SINGLE SEASON

1	**Dick Lane**	14	Rams	1952
2	**Dan Sandifer**	13	Redskins	1948
	Spec Sanders	13	Yankees	1950
	Lester Hayes	13	Raiders	1980
5	**Nine players tied with 12**			

RECORD FACT

DeAngelo Hall had a four-interception game for the Redskins on October 24, 2010. That put him in the record books, tying the mark held by 18 other players.

Interceptions

RECORD FACTS

Three players share the single-season record for interception returns for touchdowns, with four each. They are the Oilers' Ken Houston (1971), the Chiefs' Jim Kearney (1972), and the Eagles' Eric Allen (1993).

There have been 38 interception returns of 100 yards or more. Ravens defensive back Ed Reed owns the two longest returns, taking one 107 yards and another 106 yards. In 2017, the Broncos' Aqib Talib had a 103-yard pick-6.

CAREER PICK-6s

1	**Rod Woodson**	12	Steelers/49ers/Ravens/Raiders	1987–2003
2	**Darren Sharper**	11	Packers/Vikings/Saints	1997–2010
	Charles Woodson	11	Raiders/Packers	1998–2015
4	**Aqib Talib**	10	Buccaneers/Patriots/Broncos	2008–2017*
5	**Ken Houston**	9	Oilers/Redskins	1967–1980
	Aeneas Williams	9	Cardinals/Rams	1991–2004
	Deion Sanders	9	Falcons/49ers/Cowboys/Redskins/Ravens	1989–2005
8	**Eric Allen**	8	Eagles/Saints/Raiders	1988–2001
	Ronde Barber	8	Buccaneers	1997–2012
	Charles Tillman	8	Bears/Panthers	2003–2015

* active player

Defensive Fumble Recoveries

CAREER

1	**Jim Marshall**	29	Browns/Vikings	1960–1979
	Jason Taylor	29	Dolphins/Redskins/Jets	1997–2011
3	**Rickey Jackson**	28	Saints/49ers	1981–1995
4	**Cornelius Bennett**	26	Bills/Falcons/Colts	1987–2000
	Kevin Greene	26	Rams/Steelers/Panthers/49ers	1985–1999

CAREER FUMBLE RETURNS FOR TDs

1	**Jason Taylor**	6	Dolphins/Redskins/Jets	1997–2011
2	**Jessie Tuggle**	5	Falcons	1987–2000
	DeAngelo Hall	5	Falcons/Raiders/Redskins	2004–2017
4	**Link Lyman**	4	Bulldogs/Bears/Yellow Jackets	1922–1934
	Bill Thompson	4	Broncos	1969–1981
	Derrick Thomas	4	Chiefs	1989–1999
	Ronde Barber	4	Buccaneers	1997–2012
	Keith Bulluck	4	Titans/Giants	2000–2010
	Osi Umenyiora	4	Giants/Falcons	2003–2014

RECORD FACT

Don Hultz of the Vikings owns the single-season record for defensive fumble recoveries with nine in 1963.

SCOOP, SPRINT, AND SCORE

When a fumbled ball goes into the end zone, the wise thing for a defensive player to do is fall on it for a touchback. But don't tell that to Jack Tatum or Aeneas Williams. These defensive backs for the Raiders and Cardinals share the record for the longest fumble recovery for a touchdown. Each went 104 yards, end zone to end zone, for momentum-turning scores. Tatum did it against the Packers in 1972. Williams matched him against the Redskins in 2000.

◀ **Aeneas Williams**

Defensive Forced Fumbles

CAREER

1	Robert Mathis	54	Colts	2003–2016
2	Julius Peppers	52	Panthers/Bears/Packers	2002–2017*
3	John Abraham	47	Jets/Falcons/Cardinals	2000–2014
4	Jason Taylor	46	Dolphins/Redskins/Jets	1997–2011
	Dwight Freeney	46	Colts/Chargers/Cardinals/Falcons/Lions/Seahawks	2002–2017

Forced fumbles stat has been kept since 1993.

* active player

Sacks

CAREER

1	Bruce Smith	200	Bills/Redskins	1985–2003
2	Reggie White	198	Eagles/Packers/Panthers	1985–2000
3	Kevin Greene	160	Rams/Steelers/Panthers/49ers	1985–1999
4	Julius Peppers	154.5	Panthers/Bears/Packers	2002–2017*
5	Chris Doleman	150.5	Vikings/Falcons/49ers	1985–1999
6	Michael Strahan	141.5	Giants	1993–2007
7	Jason Taylor	139.5	Dolphins/Redskins/Jets	1997–2011
8	DeMarcus Ware	138.5	Cowboys/Broncos	2005–2016
9	Richard Dent	137.5	Bears/49ers/Colts/Eagles	1983–1997
	John Randle	137.5	Vikings/Seahawks	1990–2003

* active player

RECORD FACT

Deacon Jones was one of the most ferocious pass rushers in NFL history. He played for the Rams, Chargers, and Redskins from 1961 to 1974. He was known for bringing down quarterbacks and for inventing the term describing such a tackle: "sack." But Jones doesn't show up in the record books because the quarterback sack stat did not become official until 1982.

SINGLE SEASON

1	Michael Strahan	22.5	Giants	2001
2	Mark Gastineau	22	Jets	1984
	Jared Allen	22	Vikings	2011
	Justin Houston	22	Chiefs	2014
5	Reggie White	21	Eagles	1987
	Chris Doleman	21	Vikings	1989
7	Lawrence Taylor	20.5	Giants	1986
	J.J. Watt	20.5	Texans	2012
	J.J. Watt	20.5	Texans	2014
10	Derrick Thomas	20	Chiefs	1990
	DeMarcus Ware	20	Cowboys	2008

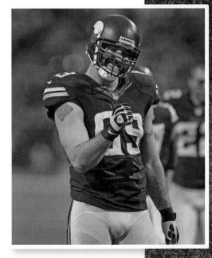

▲ Jared Allen

SACK ATTACK

Falcons defensive end Adrian Clayborn had a career day on November 12, 2017, recording an impressive six sacks. He made it a rough day for Cowboys quarterback Dak Prescott. The Seahawks' Dave Krieg, though, had a rougher day in 1990. On that day, Chiefs linebacker Derrick Thomas set the single-game sack record by bringing Krieg down behind the line of scrimmage seven times. Clayborn is one of four players with a six-sack game. Thomas is another, nearly matching his own record in 1998.

Punt Returns for Touchdowns

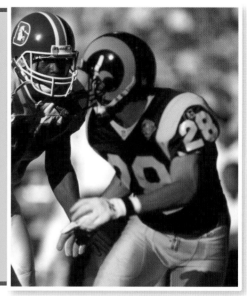

▲ Devin Hester

CAREER

1	**Devin Hester**	14	Bears/Falcons/Ravens/Seahawks	2006–2016
2	**Eric Metcalf**	10	Browns/Falcons/Chargers/Cardinals/Panthers/Redskins/Packers	1989–2002
3	**Brian Mitchell**	9	Redskins/Eagles/Giants	1990–2003
4	**Jack Christiansen**	8	Lions	1951–1958
	Rick Upchurch	8	Broncos	1975–1983
	Desmond Howard	8	Redskins/Jaguars/Packers/Raiders/Lions	1992–2002
7	**Dave Meggett**	7	Giants/Patriots/Jets	1989–1998
	Darren Sproles	7	Chargers/Saints/Eagles	2005–2017*
9	**Five players tied with 6**			

RISKY BUSINESS

Any punt that goes into the end zone is a touchback. This means that the returning team gets the ball on the 20-yard line. Returners are usually given the order to let deep punts roll into the end zone, rather than risk getting tackled in a bad field position. Not all of those players listen. In a 1994 game, the Rams' Robert Bailey caught the ball in the end zone and took off running. Eye rolls turned to excitement as Bailey scampered 103 yards for a touchdown. This remains the only punt return greater than 100 yards.

SINGLE SEASON

1	Jack Christiansen	4	Lions	1951
	Rick Upchurch	4	Broncos	1976
	Devin Hester	4	Bears	2007
	Patrick Peterson	4	Cardinals	2011
5	Eleven players tied with 3			

Kickoff Returns for Touchdowns

▲ Josh Cribbs

CAREER

1	Josh Cribbs	8	Browns/Jets/Colts	2005–2014
	Leon Washington	8	Jets/Seahawks/Patriots/Titans	2006–2014
3	Ollie Matson	6	Cardinals/Rams/Lions/Eagles	1952–1966
	Gale Sayers	6	Bears	1965–1971
	Travis Williams	6	Packers/Rams	1967–1971
	Mel Gray	6	Saints/Lions/Oilers/Titans/Eagles	1986–1997
	Dante Hall	6	Chiefs/Rams	2000–2008
8	Eleven players tied with 5			

SINGLE SEASON

1	Travis Williams	4	Packers	1967
	Cecil Turner	4	Bears	1970
3	Thirteen players tied with 3			

RECORD FACT

The record for most combined kick and punt returns for touchdowns belongs to Devin Hester. He returned 14 punts and five kickoffs for scores playing for the Bears and Falcons. He also returned the opening kickoff of Super Bowl XLI for a touchdown.

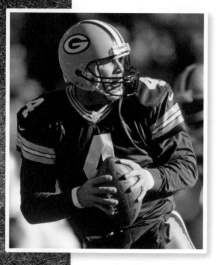

▲ Brett Favre

GAMES PLAYED

1	Morten Andersen	K	382	Saints/Falcons/Giants/Chiefs/Vikings	1982–2007
2	Gary Anderson	K	353	Steelers/Eagles/49ers/Vikings/Titans	1982–2004
3	Jeff Feagles	P	352	Patriots/Eagles/Cardinals/Seahawks/Giants	1988–2009
4	George Blanda	QB/K	340	Bears/Colts/Oilers/Raiders	1949–1975
5	Adam Vinatieri	K	337	Patriots/Colts	1996–2017*
6	Jason Hanson	K	327	Lions	1992–2012
7	Jerry Rice	WR	303	49ers/Raiders/Seahawks	1985–2004
8	John Carney	K	302	Buccaneers/Rams/Chargers/Saints/Jaguars/Chiefs/Giants	1988–2010
	Brett Favre	QB	302	Falcons/Packers/Jets/Vikings	1991–2010
10	John Kasay	K	301	Seahawks/Panthers/Saints	1991–2011

active player

IRONMEN

From week one of his rookie season in 2007 until he was injured on a play on October 22, 2017, Browns left tackle Joe Thomas didn't just start every game—he never missed a snap. He played 10,363 consecutive offensive plays. This is believed to be the longest such streak in NFL history. An arm injury eventually forced Thomas to retire, and the Browns put the number—10,363—into their ring of honor in 2018. Quarterback Brett Favre holds the streak for consecutive games started, playing 297 for three teams over 19 seasons.

CONSECUTIVE GAMES STARTED

1	Brett Favre	QB	297 (321 with playoffs)	Packers/Jets/Vikings	1992–2010
2	Jim Marshall	DE	270 (289)	Vikings	1961–1979
3	Mick Tingelhoff	C	240 (259)	Vikings	1962–1978
4	Bruce Matthews	OL	229 (244)	Oilers/Titans	1987–2002
5	Will Shields	OG	223 (231)	Chiefs	1993–2006
6	Alan Page	DT	215 (234)	Vikings/Bears	1967–1981
	Ronde Barber	DB	215 (224)	Buccaneers	1999–2012
	London Fletcher	LB	215 (221)	Rams/Bills/Redskins	2000–2013
9	Jim Otto	C	210 (223)	Raiders	1960–1974
	Eli Manning	QB	210 (222)	Giants	2004–2017

▲ Eli Manning

CONSECUTIVE GAMES PLAYED

1	Jeff Feagles	P	352 (363)	Patriots/Eagles/Cardinals/Seahawks/Giants	1998–2010
2	Brett Favre	QB	299 (323)	Packers/Jets/Vikings	1992–2010
3	Jim Marshall	DE	282 (301)	Browns/Vikings	1960–1979
4	London Fletcher	LB	256 (265)	Rams/Bills/Redskins	1998–2013
5	Shane Lechler	P	254 (264)	Raiders/Texans	2002–2017*
6	Morten Andersen	K	248 (256)	Saints/Falcons/Giants/Chiefs	1987–2002
7	Chris Gardocki	P	244 (258)	Bears/Colts/Browns/Steelers	1991–2006
8	Bill Romanowski	LB	243 (271)	49ers/Eagles/Broncos/Raiders	1988–2003
9	Mick Tingelhoff	C	240 (259)	Vikings	1962–1978
	Ryan Longwell	K	240 (253)	Packers/Vikings	1997–2012
	Ronde Barber	DB	240 (249)	Buccaneers	1998–2012

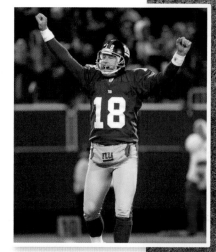

▲ Jeff Feagles

active player

All-Purpose Yards
[Rushing, Receiving, Returning]

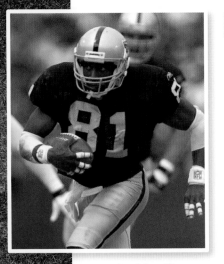

▲ Tim Brown

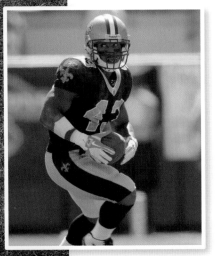

▲ Darren Sproles

CAREER

1	Jerry Rice	23,546	49ers/Raiders/Seahawks	1985–2004
2	Brian Mitchell	23,330	Redskins/Eagles/Giants	1990–2003
3	Walter Payton	21,803	Bears	1975–1987
4	Emmitt Smith	21,564	Cowboys/Cardinals	1990–2004
5	Tim Brown	19,682	Raiders/Buccaneers	1988–2004
6	Marshall Faulk	19,190	Colts/Rams	1994–2005
7	Steve Smith	19,180	Panthers/Ravens	2001–2016
8	Darren Sproles	19,155	Chargers/Saints/Eagles	2005–2017*
9	LaDainian Tomlinson	18,456	Chargers/Jets	2001–2011
10	Barry Sanders	18,308	Lions	1989–1998

active player

SINGLE SEASON

1	Darren Sproles	2,696	Saints	2011
2	Derrick Mason	2,690	Titans	2000
3	Michael Lewis	2,647	Saints	2002
4	Lionel James	2,535	Chargers	1985
5	Fred Jackson	2,516	Bills	2009
6	Josh Cribbs	2,510	Browns	2009
7	Chris Johnson	2,509	Titans	2009
8	Brian Mitchell	2,477	Redskins	1994
9	Terry Metcalf	2,462	Cardinals	1975
10	Dante Hall	2,446	Chiefs	2003

COACHING WINS

1	**Don Shula**	328	Colts/Dolphins	1963–1995
2	**George Halas**	318	Staleys/Bears	1920–1967
3	**Tom Landry**	250	Cowboys	1960–1988
	Bill Belichick	250	Browns/Patriots	1991–2017*
5	**Curly Lambeau**	226	Packers/Cardinals/Redskins	1921–1953
6	**Paul Brown**	213	Browns/Bengals	1946–1975
7	**Marty Schottenheimer**	200	Browns/Chiefs/Redskins/Chargers	1984–2006
8	**Chuck Noll**	193	Steelers	1969–1991
9	**Dan Reeves**	190	Broncos/Giants/Falcons	1981–2003
10	**Chuck Knox**	186	Rams/Bills/Seahawks	1973–1994

active coach

▲ **Don Shula**

CHAMPION COACHES

When the Patriots won Super Bowl LI in 2017, coach Bill Belichick won his fifth NFL championship. This is the most in the Super Bowl era, and tied for third all-time. Two coaches share the record for most titles won. The Bears' George Halas and the Packers' Curly Lambeau each won six championships in the league's early years. Belichick is tied with the Packers' Vince Lombardi, whose teams won five titles, including the first two Super Bowls. The Super Bowl trophy is named after Lombardi.

CHAPTER 2
Team Records

M any consider football to be the ultimate team game. Each player on the field has a job to do, whether it's blocking, tackling, throwing, catching, or running. If it's all done well, a team will have success, put points on the board, and win games—even championships! Teams can also set records. The best teams hold records for the most titles, most wins, and most points. They can also hold records for losing streaks and low-scoring seasons.

Some team records have stood for decades, such as the 73 points the Bears scored to beat the Redskins in the 1940 championship game. No team has scored more points in a single game than the Bears did that day when they won 73-0. Twenty-six years later, the Redskins were involved in the highest-scoring game of all time when they defeated the Giants 72-41. What would it be like to see those records broken?

Check out some of the top record-setting teams—both good and bad—in NFL history.

WINS *(NFL 1920–2017)*			LOSSES *(NFL 1920–2017)*		
1	Bears	749	1	Cardinals	740
2	Packers	737	2	Lions	648
3	Giants	687	3	Eagles	594
4	Steelers	619	4	Giants	585
5	Redskins	593	5	Redskins	581
6	Eagles	568	6	Bears	579
7	49ers	566	7	Packers	562
8	Rams	555	8	Rams	559
9	Lions	553	9	Steelers	552
10	Cardinals	550	10	Browns	486

▲ Chicago Bears

POINTS IN A SEASON

1	Broncos	606	2013
2	Patriots	589	2007
3	Packers	560	2011
4	Patriots	557	2012
5	Vikings	556	1998
6	Saints	547	2011
7	Rams	540	2000
	Falcons	540	2016
9	Rams	526	1999
10	Colts	522	2004

RECORD FACT

One of the stingiest defenses in NFL history belonged to the 2000 Ravens. They allowed 165 points in 16 regular-season games. That means opponents averaged just 10.3 points per game against them. Led by linebacker Ray Lewis, they went on to win Super Bowl XXXV.

MOST TEAM POINTS IN A GAME
(REGULAR SEASON)

1	Redskins	72	Nov. 27, 1966	vs. Giants
2	Rams	70	Oct. 22, 1950	vs. Colts
3	Jeffersons	66	Oct. 10, 1920	vs. Fort Porter
	Browns	66	Dec. 8, 1946	vs. Dodgers
5	Cardinals	65	Nov. 13, 1949	vs. Bulldogs
	Rams	65	Oct. 29, 1950	vs. Lions
7	Eagles	64	Nov. 6, 1934	vs. Reds
8	Cardinals	63	Oct. 17, 1948	vs. Giants
	49ers	63	Nov. 21, 1948	vs. Dodgers
	Steelers	63	Nov. 30, 1952	vs. Giants

RECORD FACT

The Buccaneers started as a franchise in 1976 and lost their first 26 games, including all 14 during their inaugural season. Two teams have gone winless for an entire season since the NFL went to a 16-game schedule in 1978. These were the 2008 Lions and the 2017 Browns.

HIGHEST TOTAL POINTS (REGULAR SEASON)

1	Redskins, 72	Giants, 41	113	Nov. 27, 1966
2	Bengals, 58	Browns, 48	106	Nov. 28, 2004
3	49ers, 63	Dodgers, 40	103	Nov. 21, 1948
4	Saints, 52	Giants, 49	101	Nov. 1, 2015
5	Seahawks, 51	Chiefs, 48 (OT)	99	Nov. 27, 1983
	Broncos, 51	Cowboys, 48	99	Oct. 6, 2013
7	Cardinals, 63	Giants, 35	98	Oct. 17, 1948
	Chargers, 54	Steelers, 44	98	Dec. 8, 1985
9	Rams, 70	Colts, 27	97	Oct. 22, 1950

CONSECUTIVE WINS
(REGULAR SEASON)

1	Colts	23	2008–2009
2	Patriots	21	2006–2008
3	Patriots	18	2003–2004
	Panthers	18	2014–2015
5	Bears	17	1933–1934
	Broncos	17	2012–2013
7	Steelers	16	2004–2005
	Dolphins	16	1971–1973
	Dolphins	16	1983–1984
10	49ers	15	1989–1990
	Packers	15	2010–2011

CONSECUTIVE LOSSES
(REGULAR SEASON)

1	Cardinals	29	1942–1945
2	Buccaneers	26	1976–1977
3	Raiders	19	1961–1962
	Lions	19	2007–2009
5	Oilers	18	1972–1973
6	Triangles	17	1927–1929
	Redskins	17	1960–1961
	Oilers	17	1982–1983
	Rams	17	2008–2009
	Browns	17	2015–2016
	Browns	17	2016–2017

BIG WINNERS

The 1972 Dolphins remain the only team to win every game of the regular season and go on to win the Super Bowl. The NFL played a 14-game schedule that season. In 2007, the Patriots looked like they were going to match that mark. They won all 16 games in the regular season and advanced to Super Bowl XLII. However, they were upset by the Giants for their only loss that year.

CHAPTER 3

Postseason Records

Every team in the NFL starts the season with the goal of making the playoffs. The ultimate prize is playing in the Super Bowl and winning a championship. The postseason has featured many outstanding and memorable performances. Some of those performances have earned long-standing spots in the record books.

In 2017, the Patriots pulled off a stunning, come-from-behind overtime victory over the Falcons to win Super Bowl LI. Quarterback Tom Brady was one of the heroes of that game, completing a playoff and Super Bowl record 43 passes. Another hero, running back James White, caught 14 of those balls, a number that also set a Super Bowl record. It wasn't a playoff record, though. That belongs to the Saints' Darren Sproles, who nabbed 15 passes during a 2012 loss to the 49ers.

Postseason records are some of the most memorable because they are set in such important games. Who could forget Jacoby Jones' 108-yard kickoff return for a touchdown for the Ravens in 2013? Or the 96-point shootout between the Cardinals and Packers in 2010?

ROMAN NUMERAL GUIDE

With the exception of Super Bowl 50, the NFL uses Roman numerals to name the Super Bowls. Super Bowl I, originally called the AFL-NFL World Championship Game, was played on January 15, 1967, following the 1966 season.

Super Bowl

PASSING TOUCHDOWNS

1	Steve Young	6	49ers	Super Bowl XXIX
2	Joe Montana	5	49ers	Super Bowl XXIV
3	Terry Bradshaw	4	Steelers	Super Bowl XIII
	Doug Williams	4	Redskins	Super Bowl XXII
	Troy Aikman	4	Cowboys	Super Bowl XXVII
	Tom Brady	4	Patriots	Super Bowl XLIX
7	Thirteen players tied with 3			

PASSING YARDS

1	Tom Brady	505	Patriots	Super Bowl LII
2	Tom Brady	466	Patriots	Super Bowl LI
3	Kurt Warner	414	Rams	Super Bowl XXXIV
4	Kurt Warner	377	Cardinals	Super Bowl XLIII
5	Nick Foles	373	Eagles	Super Bowl LII
6	Kurt Warner	365	Rams	Super Bowl XXXVI
7	Joe Montana	357	49ers	Super Bowl XXIII
	Donovan McNabb	357	Eagles	Super Bowl XXXIX
9	Tom Brady	354	Patriots	Super Bowl XXXVIII
10	Doug Williams	340	Redskins	Super Bowl XXII

1	I	1967
2	II	1968
3	III	1969
4	IV	1970
5	V	1971
6	VI	1972
7	VII	1973
8	VIII	1974
9	IX	1975
10	X	1976
11	XI	1977
12	XII	1978
13	XIII	1979
14	XIV	1980
15	XV	1981
16	XVI	1982
17	XVII	1983
18	XVIII	1984
19	XIX	1985
20	XX	1986
21	XXI	1987
22	XXII	1988
23	XXIII	1989
24	XXIV	1990
25	XXV	1991
26	XXVI	1992
27	XXVII	1993
28	XXVIII	1994
29	XXIX	1995
30	XXX	1996
31	XXXI	1997
32	XXXII	1998
33	XXXIII	1999
34	XXXIV	2000
35	XXXV	2001
36	XXXVI	2002
37	XXXVII	2003
38	XXXVIII	2004
39	XXXIX	2005
40	XL	2006
41	XLI	2007
42	XLII	2008
43	XLIII	2009
44	XLIV	2010
45	XLV	2011
46	XLVI	2012
47	XLVII	2013
48	XLVIII	2014
49	XLIX	2015
50	L, "Super Bowl 50"	2016
51	LI	2017
52	LII	2018

Super Bowl

PASSES COMPLETED

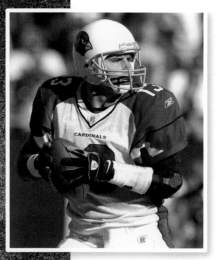

▲ Kurt Warner

1	**Tom Brady**	43	Patriots	Super Bowl LI
2	**Tom Brady**	37	Patriots	Super Bowl XLIX
3	**Peyton Manning**	34	Broncos	Super Bowl XLVIII
4	**Tom Brady**	32	Patriots	Super Bowl XXXVIII
	Drew Brees	32	Saints	Super Bowl XLIV
6	**Jim Kelly**	31	Bills	Super Bowl XXVIII
	Kurt Warner	31	Cardinals	Super Bowl XLIII
	Peyton Manning	31	Colts	Super Bowl XLIV
9	**Donovan McNabb**	30	Eagles	Super Bowl XXXIX
	Eli Manning	30	Giants	Super Bowl XLVI

LONGEST PASS *(ALL TOUCHDOWNS)*

▲ John Elway

1	**Jake Delhomme** to **Muhsin Muhammad**	85 yards	Panthers	Super Bowl XXXVIII
2	**Brett Favre** to **Antonio Freeman**	81 yards	Packers	Super Bowl XXXI
3	**Jim Plunkett** to **Kenny King**	80 yards	Raiders	Super Bowl XV
	Doug Williams to **Ricky Sanders**	80 yards	Redskins	Super Bowl XXII
	John Elway to **Rod Smith**	80 yards	Broncos	Super Bowl XXXIII
6	**David Woodley** to **Jimmy Cefalo**	76 yards	Dolphins	Super Bowl XVII
7	**Johnny Unitas** to **John Mackey**	75 yards	Colts	Super Bowl V
	Terry Bradshaw to **John Stallworth**	75 yards	Steelers	Super Bowl XIII
9	**Terry Bradshaw** to **John Stallworth**	73 yards	Steelers	Super Bowl XIV
	Kurt Warner to **Isaac Bruce**	73 yards	Rams	Super Bowl XXXIV

RUSHING YARDS

1	**Timmy Smith**	204	Redskins	Super Bowl XXII
2	**Marcus Allen**	191	Raiders	Super Bowl XVIII
3	**John Riggins**	166	Redskins	Super Bowl XVII
4	**Franco Harris**	158	Steelers	Super Bowl IX
5	**Terrell Davis**	157	Broncos	Super Bowl XXXII
6	**Larry Csonka**	145	Dolphins	Super Bowl VIII
7	**Clarence Davis**	137	Raiders	Super Bowl XI
8	**Thurman Thomas**	135	Bills	Super Bowl XXV
9	**Emmitt Smith**	132	Cowboys	Super Bowl XXVIII
10	**Michael Pittman**	124	Buccaneers	Super Bowl XXXVII

▲ Marcus Allen

LONGEST RUN

1	**Willie Parker**	75 yards (TD)	Steelers	Super Bowl XL
2	**Marcus Allen**	74 yards (TD)	Raiders	Super Bowl XVIII
3	**Tom Matte**	58 yards	Colts	Super Bowl III
	Timmy Smith	58 yards (TD)	Redskins	Super Bowl XXII
5	**Thomas Jones**	52 yards	Bears	Super Bowl XLI
6	**Larry Csonka**	49 yards	Dolphins	Super Bowl VII
7	**Alvin Garrett**	44 yards	Redskins	Super Bowl XVII
8	**John Riggins**	43 yards (TD)	Redskins	Super Bowl XVII
	Timmy Smith	43 yards	Redskins	Super Bowl XXII
10	**Wendell Tyler**	39 yards	Rams	Super Bowl XIV
	Marcus Allen	39 yards	Raiders	Super Bowl XVIII

▲ Willie Parker

Super Bowl

RECEPTIONS

1	**James White**	14	Patriots	Super Bowl LI
2	**Demaryius Thomas**	13	Broncos	Super Bowl XLVIII
3	**Dan Ross**	11	Bengals	Super Bowl XVI
	Jerry Rice	11	49ers	Super Bowl XXIII
	Deion Branch	11	Patriots	Super Bowl XXXIX
	Wes Welker	11	Patriots	Super Bowl XLII
	Shane Vereen	11	Patriots	Super Bowl XLIX
8	**Tony Nathan**	10	Dolphins	Super Bowl XIX
	Jerry Rice	10	49ers	Super Bowl XXIX
	Andre Hastings	10	Steelers	Super Bowl XXX
	Deion Branch	10	Patriots	Super Bowl XXXVIII
	Joseph Addai	10	Colts	Super Bowl XLI
	Hakeem Nicks	10	Giants	Super Bowl XLVI

▲ James White

RECEIVING YARDS

1	**Jerry Rice**	215	49ers	Super Bowl XXIII
2	**Ricky Sanders**	193	Redskins	Super Bowl XXII
3	**Isaac Bruce**	162	Rams	Super Bowl XXXIV
4	**Lynn Swann**	161	Steelers	Super Bowl X
5	**Andre Reed**	152	Bills	Super Bowl XXVII
	Rod Smith	152	Broncos	Super Bowl XXXIII
	Danny Amendola	152	Patriots	Super Bowl LII
8	**Jerry Rice**	149	49ers	Super Bowl XXIX
9	**Jerry Rice**	148	49ers	Super Bowl XXIV
10	**Deion Branch**	143	Patriots	Super Bowl XXXVIII

RECORD FACT

The Eagles' Nick Foles made history in Super Bowl LII, becoming the first quarterback to make a touchdown reception in the Super Bowl. Foles caught the pass from tight end Trey Burton on a trick play that helped the Eagles upset the Patriots.

44

DEFENSE AND SPECIAL TEAMS

The Raiders' **Rod Martin** is the only player to grab three interceptions in a Super Bowl. He picked off three passes against the Eagles in Super Bowl XV. Eleven players have had two interceptions. Only the Buccaneers' **Dwight Smith** took both picks back for touchdowns.

Four players have had three sacks in a Super Bowl: the Falcons' **Grady Jarrett**, the Panthers' **Kony Ealy**, the Cardinals' **Darnell Dockett**, and the Packers' **Reggie White**.

The longest interception return for a touchdown in a Super Bowl was 100 yards. Steelers linebacker **James Harrison** made the game-changing play at the end of the first half against the Cardinals in Super Bowl XLIII.

Jacoby Jones of the Ravens set a Super Bowl record with a 108-yard kickoff return for a touchdown in Super Bowl XLVII. In Super Bowl XXXV, the Giants' **Ron Dixon** and the Ravens' **Jermaine Lewis** made history by returning back-to-back kickoffs for touchdowns.

▲ **Reggie White**

SUPER 8

Patriots quarterback Tom Brady has appeared in eight Super Bowls, more than any other player in NFL history. He's also appeared in 37 playoff games, the most by any individual player. Brady and defensive end Charles Haley, who played for the 49ers and Cowboys, are the only two players who have won five Super Bowl rings. Bill Belichick has coached in more Super Bowls than any other person, leading the Patriots to the big game eight times.

Super Bowl

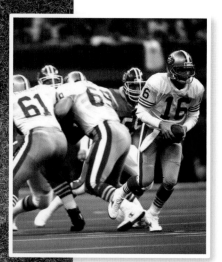

▲ 49ers, Super Bowl XXIV

MOST POINTS IN A SUPER BOWL

1	49ers	55	Super Bowl XXIV vs. Broncos
2	Cowboys	52	Super Bowl XXVII vs. Bills
3	49ers	49	Super Bowl XXIX vs. Chargers
4	Buccaneers	48	Super Bowl XXXVII vs. Raiders
5	Bears	46	Super Bowl XX vs. Patriots
6	Seahawks	43	Super Bowl XLVIII vs. Broncos
7	Redskins	42	Super Bowl XXII vs. Broncos
8	Eagles	41	Super Bowl LII vs. Patriots
9	Giants	39	Super Bowl XXI vs. Broncos
10	Raiders	38	Super Bowl XVIII vs. Redskins
	49ers	38	Super Bowl XIX vs. Dolphins

FEWEST POINTS IN A SUPER BOWL

1	Dolphins	3	Super Bowl VI vs. Cowboys
2	Vikings	6	Super Bowl IX vs. Steelers
3	Colts	7	Super Bowl III vs. Jets
	Vikings	7	Super Bowl IV vs. Chiefs
	Redskins	7	Super Bowl VII vs. Dolphins
	Vikings	7	Super Bowl VIII vs. Dolphins
	Giants	7	Super Bowl XXXV vs. Ravens
8	Broncos	8	Super Bowl XLVIII vs. Seahawks
9	Redskins	9	Super Bowl XVIII vs. Raiders
10	Eight teams tied with 10		

MOST TOTAL POINTS IN A SUPER BOWL

1	49ers, 49	Chargers, 26	75	Super Bowl XXIX
2	Eagles, 41	Patriots, 33	74	Super Bowl LII
3	Cowboys, 52	Bills, 17	69	Super Bowl XXVII
	Buccaneers, 48	Raiders, 21	69	Super Bowl XXXVII
5	Steelers, 35	Cowboys, 31	66	Super Bowl XIII
6	49ers, 55	Broncos, 10	65	Super Bowl XXIV
	Ravens, 34	49ers, 31	65	Super Bowl XLVII
8	Patriots, 34	Falcons, 28 (OT)	62	Super Bowl LI
9	Redskins, 37	Bills, 24	61	Super Bowl XXVI
	Patriots, 32	Panthers, 29	61	Super Bowl XXXVIII

FEWEST TOTAL POINTS IN A SUPER BOWL

1	Dolphins, 14	Redskins, 7	21	Super Bowl VII
2	Steelers, 16	Vikings, 6	22	Super Bowl IX
3	Jets, 16	Colts, 7	23	Super Bowl III
4	Cowboys, 24	Dolphins, 3	27	Super Bowl VI
5	Colts, 16	Cowboys, 13	29	Super Bowl V
6	Chiefs, 23	Vikings, 7	30	Super Bowl IV
7	Dolphins, 24	Vikings, 7	31	Super Bowl VIII
	Steelers, 21	Seahawks, 10	31	Super Bowl XL
	Giants, 17	Patriots, 14	31	Super Bowl XLII
10	Broncos, 24	Panthers, 10	34	Super Bowl 50

COMEBACK KIDS

The Patriots pulled off the greatest comeback in Super Bowl history in Super Bowl LI. They trailed the Falcons 28-3 with 8:36 remaining in the third quarter before scoring 25 consecutive points to tie the game with 57 seconds left in the fourth quarter. James White capped the unlikely victory with a 2-yard touchdown run in overtime that gave the Pats the 34-28 victory and their fifth Lombardi Trophy.

Super Bowl

TEAM CHAMPIONSHIPS			SUPER BOWL WINS		
1	Packers	13	1	Steelers	6
2	Bears	9	2	Cowboys	5
3	Browns	8		Patriots	5
3	Giants	8		49ers	5
5	Steelers	6	5	Giants	4
6	49ers	5		Packers	4
	Patriots	5	7	Broncos	3
	Cowboys	5		Raiders	3
	Redskins	5		Redskins	3
10	Eagles	4	10	Ravens	2
	Colts	4		Colts	2
	Lions	4		Dolphins	2

THE BIG GAME

The Super Bowl isn't just the biggest football game or the biggest sporting event in the United States. It's the biggest event in the US, period. More Americans watch the Super Bowl on television than any other program. Nine of the top 10 all-time most-watched TV programs in the US have been Super Bowls, including the top eight. Super Bowl XLIX in 2015 ranks number one, with more than 114 million viewers.

Denver Broncos, 2014

IN THE SPOTLIGHT

Two teams have lost the Super Bowl five times, although both are considered great championship franchises. The Patriots have gone to more Super Bowls than any other team. They have five victories in addition to their five losses. The Broncos have three wins and five losses. The Vikings and the Bills are both 0-4 in Super Bowl games.

SUPER BOWL APPEARANCES

1	Patriots	10
2	Broncos	8
	Steelers	8
	Cowboys	8
5	49ers	6
6	Giants	5
	Packers	5
	Raiders	5
	Redskins	5
	Dolphins	5

▲ Oakland Raiders, Super Bowl XXXVII

Playoffs

PLAYOFF APPEARANCES

1	Cowboys	32
	Packers	32
	Giants	32
4	Steelers	31
5	Vikings	29
6	Browns	28
7	Colts	27
	Rams	28
9	49ers	26
10	Patriots	25
	Bears	25
	Eagles	25

MOST POINTS IN A PLAYOFF GAME

1	Bears	73	Dec. 8, 1940	vs. Redskins
2	Jaguars	62	Jan. 15, 2000	vs. Dolphins
3	Lions	59	Dec. 29, 1957	vs. Browns
4	Eagles	58	Dec. 30, 1995	vs. Lions
5	Browns	56	Dec. 26, 1954	vs. Lions
	Raiders	56	Dec. 21, 1969	vs. Oilers
7	49ers	55	Jan. 28, 1990	vs. Broncos*
8	Cowboys	52	Dec. 24, 1967	vs. Browns
	Cowboys	52	Jan. 31, 1993	vs. Bills*
10	Four teams tied with 51			

Super Bowl

▲ Seahawks

MOST TOTAL POINTS IN A PLAYOFF GAME

1	Cardinals, 51	Packers, 45	96	Jan. 10, 2010
2	Eagles, 58	Lions, 37	95	Dec. 30, 1995
3	Colts, 45	Chiefs, 44	89	Jan. 4, 2014
4	Jaguars, 45	Steelers, 42	87	Jan. 14, 2018
5	Rams, 49	Vikings, 37	86	Jan. 16, 2000
6	Chargers, 41	Dolphins, 38 (OT)	79	Jan. 2, 1982
	Bills, 41	Oilers, 38 (OT)	79	Jan. 3, 1993
8	Bills, 44	Dolphins, 34	78	Jan. 12, 2012
9	49ers, 39	Giants, 38	77	Jan. 5, 2003
	Seahawks, 41	Saints, 36	77	Jan. 8, 2011

PASSES COMPLETED IN A SINGLE PLAYOFF GAME

1	**Tom Brady**	43	Patriots	Feb. 5, 2017
2	**Drew Brees**	40	Saints	Jan. 14, 2012
3	**Drew Brees**	39	Saints	Jan. 8, 2011
4	**Tom Brady**	37	Patriots	Feb. 1, 2015
	Ben Roethlisberger	37	Steelers	Jan. 14, 2018
6	**Warren Moon**	36	Oilers	Jan. 3, 1993
7	**Tom Brady**	35	Patriots	Jan. 13, 2018
8	**Matt Schaub**	34	Texans	Jan. 13, 2013
	Peyton Manning	34	Broncos	Feb. 2, 2014
10	**Six players tied with 33**			

▲ **Warren Moon**

PASSING YARDS IN A SINGLE PLAYOFF GAME

1	**Tom Brady**	505	Patriots	Feb. 4, 2018
2	**Bernie Kosar**	489	Browns	Jan. 3, 1987
3	**Ben Roethlisberger**	469	Steelers	Jan. 14, 2018
4	**Drew Brees**	466	Saints	Jan. 7, 2012
	Tom Brady	466	Patriots	Feb. 5, 2017
6	**Drew Brees**	462	Saints	Jan. 14, 2012
7	**Peyton Manning**	458	Colts	Jan. 9, 2005
8	**Andrew Luck**	443	Colts	Jan. 4, 2014
9	**Dan Fouts**	433	Chargers	Jan. 2, 1982
10	**Kelly Holcomb**	429	Browns	Jan. 5, 2003

RECORD FACT

Steve Young owns the record for the most pass attempts in a single playoff game. The 49ers quarterback threw the ball 65 times in a loss to the Packers on January 6, 1996.

Playoffs

LONGEST PASS

1	**Trent Dilfer** to **Shannon Sharpe**	96 yards (TD)	Ravens	Jan. 14, 2001
2	**Troy Aikman** to **Alvin Harper**	94 yards (TD)	Cowboys	Jan. 8, 1995
3	**Daryle Lamonica** to **Elbert Dubenion**	93 yards (TD)	Bills	Dec. 28, 1963
4	**Brett Favre** to **Donald Driver**	90 yards (TD)	Packers	Jan. 20, 2008
5	**George Blanda** to **Billy Cannon**	88 yards (TD)	Oilers	Jan. 1, 1961
	Drew Brees to **Reggie Bush**	88 yards (TD)	Saints	Jan. 21, 2007
7	**Peyton Manning** to **Brandon Stokley**	87 yards (TD)	Colts	Jan. 4, 2004
8	**Don Meredith** to **Bob Hayes**	86 yards (TD)	Cowboys	Dec. 24, 1967
	Jeff Hostetler to **Tim Brown**	86 yards (TD)	Raiders	Jan. 15, 1994
	Cam Newton to **Corey Brown**	86 yards (TD)	Panthers	Jan. 24, 2016

TOUCHDOWN PASSES IN A SINGLE PLAYOFF GAME

1	**Daryle Lamonica**	6	Raiders	Dec. 21, 1969
	Steve Young	6	49ers	Jan. 29, 1995
	Tom Brady	6	Patriots	Jan. 14, 2012
4	**Eight players tied with 5**			

INTERCEPTIONS THROWN IN A SINGLE PLAYOFF GAME

1	**Frank Filchock**	6	Giants	Dec. 15, 1946
	Bobby Layne	6	Lions	Dec. 26, 1954
	Norm Van Brocklin	6	Rams	Dec. 26, 1955
	Brett Favre	6	Packers	Jan. 20, 2002
5	**Fourteen players tied with 5**			

RUSHING YARDS IN A SINGLE PLAYOFF GAME

1	**Eric Dickerson**	248	Rams	Jan. 4, 1986
2	**Lamar Smith**	209	Dolphins	Dec. 30, 2000
3	**Keith Lincoln**	206	Chargers	Jan. 5, 1964
4	**Timmy Smith**	204	Redskins	Jan. 31, 1988
5	**Lawrence McCutcheon**	202	Rams	Dec. 27, 1975
	Freeman McNeil	202	Jets	Jan. 9, 1983
7	**Ryan Grant**	201	Packers	Jan. 12, 2008
8	**Terrell Davis**	199	Broncos	Jan. 9, 1999
9	**Steve Van Buren**	196	Eagles	Dec. 18, 1949
10	**Wilbert Montgomery**	194	Eagles	Jan. 11, 1981

LONGEST RUN

1	**Fred Taylor**	90 yards (TD)	Jaguars	Jan. 15, 2000
2	**Ray Rice**	83 yards (TD)	Ravens	Jan. 10, 2010
3	**Roger Craig**	80 (TD)	49ers	Jan. 1, 1989
	Charlie Garner	80 (TD)	Raiders	Jan. 12, 2002
5	**Curtis Martin**	78 (TD)	Patriots	Jan. 5, 1997
6	**Willie Parker**	75 (TD)	Steelers	Feb. 5, 2006
7	**Marcus Allen**	74 (TD)	Raiders	Jan. 22, 1984
	Adrian Murrell	74	Cardinals	Jan. 2, 1999
9	**Felix Jones**	73 (TD)	Cowboys	Jan. 9, 2010
	LeGarrette Blount	73 (TD)	Patriots	Jan. 11, 2014

RECORD FACT

In 1994, 49ers running back Ricky Watters set the record for the most rushing touchdowns in a single playoff game, scoring five times against the Giants. His 30 points scored that day were also a playoff record.

KICKING WHEN IT COUNTS

Adam Vinatieri is one of the best clutch kickers to play in the NFL. He was the first kicker to win four Super Bowl rings. In two of those championships, he kicked the winning field goal in the closing seconds of the game. No kicker has made more playoff kicks than Vinatieri. Playing for the Patriots and the Colts, Vinatieri has booted 56 field goals between the 1996 and 2017 seasons.

Playoffs

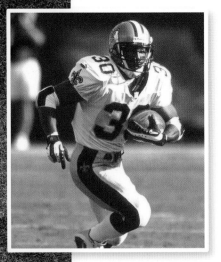

▲ Chad Morton

RECEPTIONS IN A SINGLE PLAYOFF GAME

1	Darren Sproles	15	Saints	Jan. 14, 2012
2	James White	14	Patriots	Feb. 5, 2017
3	Kellen Winslow	13	Chargers	Jan. 2, 1982
	Thurman Thomas	13	Bills	Jan. 6, 1990
	Shannon Sharpe	13	Broncos	Jan. 9, 1994
	Chad Morton	13	Saints	Jan. 6, 2001
	T.Y. Hilton	13	Colts	Jan. 4, 2014
	Demaryius Thomas	13	Broncos	Feb. 2, 2014
9	Five players tied with 12			

RECORD FACT

Players have caught three touchdown passes in a single playoff game 17 times. The most recent was Randall Cobb of the Packers on January 8, 2017, against the Giants. Jerry Rice is the only player to accomplish the feat more than once, doing it three times.

RECEIVING YARDS IN A SINGLE PLAYOFF GAME

1	Eric Moulds	240	Bills	Jan. 2, 1999
2	Anthony Carter	227	Vikings	Jan. 9, 1988
3	T.Y. Hilton	224	Colts	Jan. 4, 2014
4	Reggie Wayne	221	Colts	Jan. 9, 2005
5	Steve Smith	218	Panthers	Jan. 15, 2006
6	Jerry Rice	215	49ers	Jan. 22, 1989
7	Calvin Johnson	211	Lions	Jan. 7, 2012
8	Demaryius Thomas	204	Broncos	Jan. 8, 2012
9	Tom Fears	198	Rams	Dec. 17, 1950
10	Ricky Sanders	193	Redskins	Jan. 31, 1988

▲ Aeneas Williams

DEFENSE

The Oilers' **Vernon Perry** intercepted four passes against the Chargers during a playoff game on December 29, 1979. Seven players have had three-interception games.

The Rams' **Aeneas Williams** (2002) and the Buccaneers' **Dwight Smith** (2003) are the only players to return two interceptions for touchdowns in a single playoff game.

The longest interception return for a touchdown in a playoff game was 101 yards by the Packers' **George Teague** against the Lions on January 8, 1994.

The Patriots' **Willie McGinest** holds the record for sacks in a single playoff game. He brought down Jaguars quarterbacks 4.5 times on January 7, 2006. The Bears' **Richard Dent** and the Redskins' **Rich Milot** are next on the list, with 3.5 sacks.

McGinest has more career playoff sacks than any other player, racking up 16 between 1994 and 2008.

The Steelers' **Jack Lambert** recovered three Raiders fumbles during a playoff game on January 4, 1976.

RECORD FACT

On January 15, 2017, Steelers kicker Chris Boswell made six field goals in a playoff win over the Chiefs. That broke the record of five field goals in a single game, which had been done 10 times, twice by Adam Vinatieri.

CHAPTER 4
Around the Field

There's an old saying that records were made to be broken. That also goes for records that many believe to be unbreakable.

Legendary quarterback Johnny Unitas went on a streak of 47 games in which he threw at least one touchdown pass. For a span of four years—from December 9, 1956, through December 4, 1960—opposing defenses were unable to shut down the Colts passer. When the streak ended, it was considered one of the greatest records in football.

But, more than five decades later, along came Drew Brees. In 2012, the Saints superstar QB passed Unitas and reached 54 straight games with a touchdown pass before being stopped. Tom Brady (52) and Peyton Manning (51) also passed Unitas. However, they weren't able to catch Brees.

What other unbreakable records are out there just waiting to be challenged? The Bills' 32-point comeback against the Oilers? Norm Van Brocklin's 554-yard passing game?

GREATEST COMEBACKS *(REGULAR SEASON)*

1	49ers, 38	Saints, 35	**49ers trailed by 28 (35-7)**	Dec. 7, 1980
2	Bills, 37	Colts, 35	**Bills trailed by 26 (26-0)**	Sept. 21, 1997
3	Browns, 29	Titans, 28	**Browns trailed by 25 (28-3)**	Oct. 5, 2014
	Cardinals, 31	Buccaneers, 28	**Cardinals trailed by 25 (28-3)**	Nov. 8, 1987
5	**Teams have rallied from 24-point deficits 16 times.**			

▲ Browns vs. Titans

GREATEST COMEBACKS *(POSTSEASON)*

1	Bills, 41	Oilers, 38	**Bills trailed by 32 (35-3)**	Jan. 3, 1993
2	Colts, 45	Chiefs, 44	**Colts trailed by 28 (38-10)**	Jan. 4, 2014
3	Patriots, 34	Falcons, 28	**Patriots trailed by 25 (28-3)**	Feb. 5, 2017*
4	49ers, 39	Giants, 38	**49ers trailed by 24 (38-14)**	Jan. 5, 2003
5	Lions, 31	49ers, 27	**Lions trailed by 20 (27-7)**	Dec. 22, 1957

* Super Bowl

UNBREAKABLE RECORDS

A football field is 100 yards long—120 if you include the two end zones. The longest possible play is 109 yards. It must start in the back of one end zone and end at the other goal line for a touchdown. There have been two 109-yard plays in NFL history. The first was by the Chargers' **Antonio Cromartie**. He returned a missed field goal on November 4, 2007. Six years later, on October 27, 2013, the Vikings' **Cordarrelle Patterson** matched that with a 109-kickoff return for a score.

▲ Cordarrelle Patterson

▲ Devin Hester

▲ Antonio Cromartie

The career record holder for non-offensive touchdowns (defense and special teams) is **Devin Hester**. He scored 20 times for four teams from 2006 to 2016.

In 1943, the Redskins' **Sammy Baugh** showed he could do it all. "Slingin' Sammy" led the NFL in passing on offense, interceptions on defense, and punting on special teams.

The longest punt in NFL history went 98 yards. The Jets' **Steve O'Neal** booted the record-breaker on September 21, 1969. The play started on the Jets' 1-yard line. O'Neal punted out of his own end zone. The ball went untouched before rolling to a stop on the opposite 1-yard line.

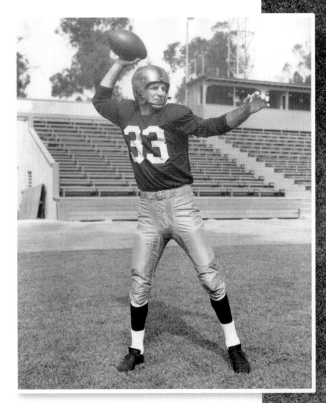

▲ **Sammy Baugh**

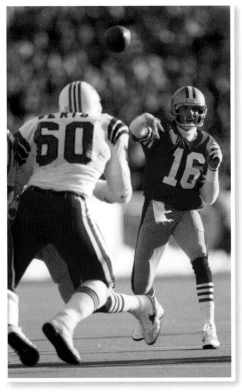

▲ **Joe Montana**

The Rams' **Norm Van Brocklin** passed for 554 yards in a game on September 28, 1951. The single-game record has stood for more than six decades.

Between 1988 and 1990, the **49ers** won a record 18 consecutive games on the road.

George Blanda played in the NFL for a record 26 seasons, finally retiring at the age of 48. The quarterback and kicker played for the Bears, Colts, Oilers, and Raiders.

▲ Colts vs. Chiefs, January 7, 1996

COLDEST GAMES

1	**Packers 21, Cowboys 17**	-13 degrees (wind chill -36)	Dec. 31, 1967	at Green Bay
2	**Bengals 27, Chargers 7**	-9 degrees (wind chill -34)	Jan. 10, 1982	at Cincinnati
3	**Colts 10, Chiefs 7**	-6 degrees (wind chill NA)	Jan. 7, 1996	at Kansas City
	Seahawks 10, Vikings 9	-6 degrees (wind chill -25)	Jan. 10, 2016	at Minnesota
5	**Raiders 14, Browns 12**	-5 degrees (wind chill -20)	Jan. 4, 1981	at Cleveland
6	**Giants 23, Packers 20**	-4 degrees (wind chill -24)	Jan. 20, 2008	at Green Bay
7	**Vikings 23, Bears 10**	-2 degrees (wind chill -19)	Dec. 3, 1972	at Minnesota
8	**Packers 23, Vikings 7**	0 degrees (wind chill -15)	Dec. 10, 1972	at Minnesota
	Packers 28, Raiders 0	0 degrees (wind chill -15)	Dec. 26, 1993	at Green Bay
	Bills 29, Raiders 23	0 degrees (wind chill -20)	Jan. 15, 1994	at Buffalo

OLDEST TEAMS

1	Cardinals	1898 (started as the Morgan Athletic Club in Chicago)
2	Packers	1919 (oldest team still in the same city)
3	Bears	1920 (started as the Decatur Staleys)
4	Giants	1925
5	Lions	1930
6	Redskins	1932
7	Eagles	1933
	Steelers	1933
9	Rams	1937
10	49ers	1946
	Browns	1946

NEWEST TEAMS

1	Texans	2002
2	Ravens	1996
3	Jaguars	1995
	Panthers	1995
5	Buccaneers	1976
	Seahawks	1976
7	Bengals	1968
8	Saints	1967
9	Dolphins	1966
	Falcons	1966

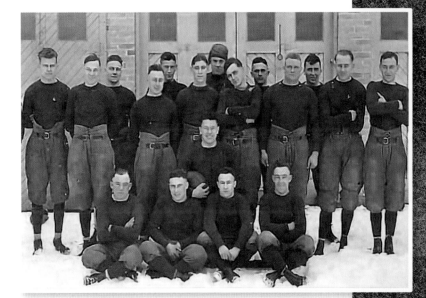

▲ 1919 Green Bay Packers

▲ Houston Texans

RECORD FACT

The oldest stadium in the NFL is Soldier Field in Chicago, the current home of the Bears. It opened in 1924. The Bears moved there in 1971.

Read More

Frederick, Shane. *Football is a Numbers Game: A Fan's Guide to Stats.* North Mankato, Minn.: Capstone Press, 2018.

Hetrick, Hans. *Football's Record Breakers.* North Mankato, Minn.: Capstone Press, 2017.

Morey, Allan. *Football Records.* Incredible Sports Records. Minneapolis, Minn.: Bellwether Media, Inc., 2018.

Internet Sites

Use FactHound to find Internet sites related to this book.

Visit *www.facthound.com*

Just type in 9781543554618 and go.

Check out projects, games and lots more at
www.capstonekids.com

Index

Abraham, John, 28
Addai, Joseph, 44
Aikman, Troy, 41, 52
Akers, David, 21, 23, 24
Alexander, Shaun, 14, 15, 21, 22
Allen, Eric, 26
Allen, Jared, 29
Allen, Keenan, 17
Allen, Marcus, 14, 21, 43, 53

Allen, Terry, 15
Amendola, Danny, 44
Andersen, Morten, 20, 23, 32, 33
Anderson, Flipper, 18
Anderson, Gary, 20, 21, 23, 32
Anderson, Mike, 14
Arizona Cardinals, 9, 12, 13, 14, 16, 17, 18, 19, 20, 21, 23, 24, 25, 26, 27, 28, 30, 31, 32, 33, 34, 35, 37, 38, 39, 40, 41, 42, 45, 50, 53, 57, 61
Atlanta Falcons, 7, 8, 10, 12, 13, 16, 17, 18, 19, 20, 21, 23, 26, 27, 28, 29, 30, 31, 32, 33, 35, 37, 40, 45, 47, 57, 61

Bailey, Robert, 30
Bakken, Jim, 24
Baltimore Ravens, 12, 13, 14, 16, 17, 20, 23, 25, 26, 30, 34, 37, 40, 45, 46, 47, 48, 52, 53, 61
Barber, Ronde, 26, 27, 33
Barber, Tiki, 15
Baugh, Sammy, 59
Belichick, Bill, 35, 45
Bennett, Cornelius, 26
Benton, Jim, 18
Bettis, Jerome, 13
Bironas, Rob, 24
Blanda, George, 8, 12, 20, 32, 52, 59
Bledsoe, Drew, 11

Blount, LeGarrette, 53
Boldin, Anquan, 16
Boniol, Chris, 24
Boswell, Chris, 55
Box, Cloyce, 18
Bradshaw, Terry, 41, 42
Brady, Tom, 5, 7, 8, 9, 10, 11, 40, 41, 42, 45, 51, 52, 56
Branch, Deion, 44
Brees, Drew, 7, 8, 9, 10, 42, 51, 52, 56
Brown, Antonio, 16, 17, 18
Brown, Corey, 52
Brown, Jim, 13, 14, 21
Brown, Paul, 35
Brown, Tim, 16, 17, 19, 34, 52

Brown, Troy, 17
Bruce, Isaac, 17, 18, 42, 44
Bryant, Matt, 21
Buffalo Bills, 13, 14, 16, 17, 19, 21, 22, 26, 28, 33, 34, 35, 42, 43, 44, 46, 47, 49, 50, 52, 54, 56, 57, 60
Bulluck, Keith, 27
Burk, Adrian, 8
Bush, Reggie, 52
Butker, Harrison, 23

Campbell, Earl, 13
Cannon, Billy, 52
Carney, John, 20, 23, 32
Carolina Panthers, 12, 15, 17, 20, 23, 26, 28, 30, 32, 34, 39, 42, 45, 47, 52, 54, 61
Carr, Derek, 9
Carter, Anthony, 54
Carter, Cris, 16, 19, 21
Cefalo, Jimmy, 42
Charles, Jamaal, 14
Chicago Bears, 8, 12, 13, 14, 20, 26, 27, 28, 30, 31, 32, 33, 34, 35, 36, 37, 39, 43, 46, 48, 50, 55, 59, 60, 61
Christiansen, Jack, 30, 31
Cincinnati Bengals, 14, 15, 16, 17, 19, 21, 24, 25, 35, 38, 44, 60, 61
Clayborn, Adrian, 29
Clayton, Mark, 19
Cleveland Browns, 12, 13, 14, 20, 21, 23, 26, 30, 31, 32, 33, 34, 35, 37, 38, 39, 48, 50, 51, 57, 60, 61
Cousins, Kirk, 11
Craig, Roger, 53
Cribbs, Josh, 31, 34
Cromartie, Antonio, 58
Csonka, Larry, 43
Cundiff, Billy, 24

Dallas Cowboys, 11, 12, 13, 14, 15, 16, 17, 19, 21, 22, 24, 26, 28, 29, 34, 35, 38, 41, 43, 45, 46, 47, 48, 49, 50, 52, 53, 60
Davis, Clarence, 43
Davis, Terrell, 13, 15, 22, 43, 53
Dawson, Phil, 20, 23
Delhomme, Jake, 42
Dempsey, Tom, 24
Dent, Richard, 28, 55
Denver Broncos, 5, 7, 8, 9, 10, 12, 13, 14, 15, 17, 20, 22, 23, 24, 26, 27, 28, 30, 31, 33, 35, 37, 38, 39, 42, 43, 44, 46, 47, 48, 49, 50, 51, 53, 54

Detroit Lions, 7, 9, 12, 13, 14, 15, 16, 18, 20, 23, 25, 28, 30, 31, 32, 34, 37, 38, 39, 48, 50, 52, 54, 55, 57, 61
Dickerson, Eric, 13, 53
Dilfer, Trent, 52
Dillon, Corey, 14, 15
Dixon, Ron, 45
Dockett, Darnell, 45
Doleman, Chris, 28, 29
Dorow, Al, 12
Dorsett, Tony, 13, 15
Driver, Donald, 52
Dubenion, Elbert, 52

Elam, Jason, 20, 23, 24
Elway, John, 8, 10, 42
Esiason, Boomer, 9

Faulk, Marshall, 14, 21, 22, 34
Favre, Brett, 5, 7, 8, 10, 12, 32, 33, 42, 52
Feagles, Jeff, 32, 33
Fears, Tom, 17, 54
Filchock, Frank, 52
Fitzgerald, Larry, 16, 17, 19
Fletcher, London, 33
Foles, Nick, 8, 41, 44
Fouts, Dan, 51
Freeman, Antonio, 42
Freeney, Dwight, 28

Gage, Bob, 15
Gaines, Clark, 17
Gannon, Rich, 11
Gano, Graham, 52
Gardocki, Chris, 33
Garner, Charlie, 53
Garrett, Alvin, 43
Gastineau, Mark, 29
Gonzalez, Tony, 16, 17, 19
Gore, Frank, 13
Gostkowski, Stephen, 21, 23
Gould, Robbie, 23
Graham, Shayne, 24
Grant, Ryan, 53
Gray, Mel, 31
Green, Ahman, 13, 15
Greenbay Packers, 5, 7, 8, 10, 11, 12, 13, 15, 19, 20, 21, 25, 26, 27, 28, 30, 31, 32, 33, 35, 37, 39, 40, 42, 45, 48, 49, 50, 51, 52, 53, 54, 55, 60, 61
Greene, Kevin, 26, 28
Groman, Bill, 19
Gronkowski, Rob, 19

Hadl, John, 12
Halas, George, 35
Haley, Charles, 45

Hall, Dante, 31, 34
Hall, DeAngelo, 25, 27
Hanson, Jason, 20, 23, 32
Hardy, Jim, 12
Harper, Alvin, 52
Harris, Franco, 43
Harrison, James, 45
Harrison, Jerome, 14
Harrison, Marvin, 16, 17, 18, 19, 21
Hart, Jim, 12
Hastings, Andre, 44
Hayes, Bob, 52
Hayes, Lester, 25
Hearst, Garrison, 15
Hennigan, Charley, 18
Hester, David, 30, 31, 58, 59
Hilton, T.Y., 54
Hirsch, Elroy, 19
Hoernschemeyer, Bob, 15
Holcomb, Kelly, 51
Holmes, Priest, 15, 21, 22
Holt, Torry, 18
Hornung, Paul, 20, 21
Hostetler, Jeff, 52
Houston, Justin, 29
Houston, Ken, 26
Houston Oilers, 8, 9, 10, 11, 12, 13, 18, 19, 20, 26, 31, 32, 33, 39, 50, 51, 52, 55, 56, 57, 59
Houston Texans, 9, 11, 25, 29, 33, 51, 61
Howard, Desmond, 30
Hultz, Don, 27
Hutson, Don, 19

Indianapolis Colts, 5, 7, 8, 10, 12, 13, 14, 15, 16, 17, 18, 19, 20, 21, 23, 26, 28, 31, 32, 33, 34, 35, 37, 38, 39, 42, 43, 44, 46, 47, 48, 50, 51, 52, 53, 54, 56, 57, 59, 60

Jackson, Fred, 34
Jackson, Rickey, 26
Jacksonville Jaguars, 17, 18, 20, 23, 30, 32, 50, 53, 55, 61
James, Lionel, 34
Janikowski, Sebastian, 23, 24
Jarrett, Grady, 45
Johnson, Calvin, 16, 18, 54
Johnson, Chris, 13, 34
Jones, Felix, 53
Jones, Jacoby, 40, 45
Jones, Julio, 16, 18
Jones, Thomas, 43

Kansas City Chiefs, 8, 10, 14, 15, 16, 17, 18, 19, 20, 21, 22, 23, 24, 26, 27, 29, 31, 32, 33, 34, 35, 38, 46, 47, 50, 55, 57, 60
Kapp, Joe, 8
Karlis, Rich, 24
Kasay, John, 20, 23, 32
Kelly, Jim, 42
Kerney, Jim, 26
King, Kenny, 42
Knox, Chuck, 35
Krause, Paul, 25
Krieg, Dave, 29

Lambeau, Curly, 35
Lambert, Jack, 55
Lamonica, Daryle, 52
Landry, Tom, 35
Lane, Dick, 25
Layne, Bobby, 52
Lechler, Shane, 33
Lewis, Jamal, 13, 14
Lewis, Jermaine, 45
Lewis, Michael, 34
Lincoln, Keith, 53
Longwell, Ryan, 33
Los Angeles Chargers, 7, 8, 10, 11, 12, 13, 14, 15, 17, 19, 20, 21, 22, 23, 28, 30, 32, 34, 35, 38, 46, 47, 50, 51, 53, 54, 55, 58, 60
Lott, Ronnie, 25
Luck, Andrew, 51
Luckman, Sid, 8, 12
Lyman, Link, 27

Mackey, John, 42
Manning, Eli, 7, 8, 10, 11, 33, 42
Manning, Peyton, 5, 7, 8, 9, 10, 12, 42, 51, 52, 56
Mare, Olindo, 23
Marino, Dan, 5, 7, 8, 9, 10, 12
Marshall, Brandon, 17
Marshall, Jim, 26, 33
Martin, Curtis, 13, 53
Martin, Doug, 14
Martin, Rod, 45
Mason, Derrick, 34
Mathis, Robert, 28
Matson, Ollie, 31
Matte, Tom, 43
Matthews, Bruce, 33
McCardell, Keenan, 17
McCutcheon, Lawrence, 53
McGinest, Willie, 55
McNabb, Donovan, 41, 42
McNeil, Freeman, 53
Meggett, Dave, 30
Meredith, Don, 52

Metcalf, Eric, 30
Metcalf, Terry, 34
Miami Dolphins, 5, 7, 8, 9, 10, 12, 15, 16, 19, 21, 23, 26, 27, 28, 35, 39, 42, 43, 44, 46, 47, 48, 49, 50, 52, 53, 61
Miller, Lamar, 15
Milot, Rich, 55
Minnesota Vikings, 7, 8, 10, 12, 13, 14, 15, 16, 17, 19, 20, 21, 23, 24, 25, 26, 27, 28, 29, 32, 33, 37, 46, 47, 49, 50, 54, 58, 60
Mitchell, Brian, 30, 34
Montana, Joe, 41, 59
Montgomery, Wilbert, 53
Moon, Warren, 8, 9, 10, 11, 51
Moore, Herman, 16, 18
Morris, Joe, 15
Morton, Chad, 54
Moseley, Mark, 21
Moss, Randy, 17, 19, 21, 22
Moulds, Eric, 54
Muhammad, Muhsin, 42
Murray, DeMarco, 14
Murrell, Adrian, 53

Nathan, Tony, 44
Nevers, Ernie, 20
New England Patriots, 5, 7, 8, 9, 10, 11, 12, 13, 16, 17, 18, 19, 20, 21, 22, 23, 26, 30, 31, 32, 33, 35, 37, 39, 40, 41, 42, 44, 45, 46, 47, 48, 49, 50, 51, 52, 53, 54, 55, 57
New Orleans Saints, 7, 8, 9, 10, 14, 20, 23, 24, 25, 26, 30, 31, 32, 33, 34, 37, 38, 40, 42, 50, 51, 52, 54, 56, 57, 61
Newton, Cam, 15, 52
New York Giants, 7, 8, 9, 10, 11, 12, 15, 18, 20, 23, 25, 27, 28, 29, 30, 32, 33, 34, 35, 36, 37, 38, 39, 42, 44, 45, 46, 47, 48, 49, 50, 52, 53, 54, 57, 60, 61
New York Jets, 7, 8, 10, 11, 12, 13, 14, 17, 21, 25, 26, 27, 28, 29, 30, 31, 32, 33, 34, 46, 47, 53, 59
New York Yankees, 25
Nicks, Hakeem, 44
Noll, Chuck, 35

Oakland Raiders, 9, 11, 12, 13, 14, 16, 17, 19, 20, 21, 23, 24, 25, 26, 27, 30, 32, 33, 34, 39, 42, 43, 45, 46, 47, 48, 49, 50, 52, 53, 55, 59, 60
O'Neal, Steve, 59

Otto, Jim, 33
Owens, Terrell, 16, 17, 19, 21

Page, Alan, 33
Paige, Stephone, 18
Parker, Willie, 43, 53
Patterson, Cordarrelle, 58
Payton, Walter, 13, 14, 34
Peppers, Julius, 28
Perry, Vernon, 55
Peterson, Adrian, 13, 14
Peterson, Patrick, 31
Philadelphia Eagles, 5, 8, 12, 16, 17, 19, 20, 21, 23, 26, 28, 29, 30, 31, 32, 33, 34, 37, 38, 41, 42, 44, 45, 46, 47, 48, 50, 53, 61
Pickens, Carl, 19
Pittman, Michael, 43
Pittsburg Steelers, 7, 8, 9, 10, 11, 13, 15, 16, 17, 18, 20, 23, 25, 26, 28, 32, 33, 35, 37, 38, 39, 41, 42, 43, 44, 45, 46, 47, 48, 49, 50, 51, 53, 55, 61
Plunkett, Jim, 42
Prater, Matt, 24

Rackers, Neil, 23
Randle, John, 28
Randle, Sonny, 17
Reed, Andre, 44
Reed, Ed, 25, 26
Reeves, Dan, 35
Rice, Jerry, 6, 16, 17, 18, 19, 21, 22, 32, 34, 44, 54
Rice, Ray, 53
Riggins, John, 14, 15, 22, 43
Riley, Ken, 25
Rivers, Philip, 7, 8, 10, 11
Rodgers, Aaron, 5, 7, 11
Roethlisberger, Ben, 7, 8, 9, 10, 11, 51
Romanowski, Bill, 33
Romo, Tony, 11
Ross, Dan, 44
Ryan, Matt, 10

Sanders, Barry, 13, 14, 34
Sanders, Deion, 26
Sanders, Ricky, 42, 44, 54
Sanders, Spec, 25
Sandifer, Dan, 25
San Francisco 49ers, 6, 12, 13, 15, 16, 17, 18, 19, 20, 21, 22, 23, 24, 25, 26, 28, 32, 33, 34, 37, 38, 39, 40, 41, 44, 45, 46, 47, 48, 49, 50, 51, 52, 53, 54, 57, 59, 61
Santos, Cairo, 24
Sayers, Gale, 20, 31

Schaub, Matt, 9, 11, 51
Schottenheimer, Marty, 35
Seattle Seahawks, 5, 8, 10, 14, 15, 16, 17, 19, 20, 21, 22, 23, 28, 29, 30, 31, 32, 33, 34, 35, 38, 46, 47, 50, 60, 61
Sharper, Darren, 22, 25, 26
Sharpe, Shannon, 52, 54
Sharpe, Sterling, 19
Shaw, Bob, 19
Shields, Will, 33
Shula, Don, 35
Simms, Phil, 9
Simpson, O.J., 13, 14, 22
Smith, Bruce, 28
Smith, Dwight, 45, 55
Smith, Emmitt, 5, 13, 14, 15, 21, 22, 34, 43
Smith, Jimmy, 18
Smith, Lamar, 53
Smith, Rod, 42, 44
Smith, Steve, 17, 34, 54
Smith, Timmy, 43, 53
Snead, Norm, 12
Spavital, Jim, 15
Sproles, Darren, 30, 34, 40, 54
Stabler, Ken, 12
Stafford, Matthew, 7, 9
Stallworth, John, 42
St. Louis Rams, 2, 5, 7, 9, 12, 13, 14, 17, 18, 19, 20, 21, 22, 23, 24, 25, 26, 28, 30, 31, 32, 33, 34, 35, 37, 38, 39, 41, 42, 43, 44, 50, 52, 53, 54, 55, 59, 61
Stokley, Brandon, 52
Stover, Matt, 20, 23
Stoyanovich, Pete, 52
Strahan, Michael, 28, 29
Swann, Lynn, 44

Talib, Aqib, 26
Tampa Bay Buccaneers, 12, 14, 16, 17, 19, 20, 23, 26, 27, 32, 33, 34, 38, 39, 43, 45, 46, 47, 55, 57, 61
Tarkenton, Fran, 7, 12
Tatum, Jack, 27
Taylor, Chester, 15
Taylor, Fred, 53
Taylor, Jason, 26, 27, 28
Taylor, John, 18
Teague, George, 55
Tennessee Titans, 12, 13, 17, 19, 20, 21, 23, 24, 27, 31, 32, 33, 34, 57
Testaverde, Vinny, 11, 12
Thomas, Demaryius, 44, 54
Thomas, Derrick, 27, 29
Thomas, Joe, 32

Thomas, Thurman, 43, 54
Thompson, Bill, 27
Tillman, Charles, 26
Tingelhoff, Mick, 33
Tittle, Y.A., 8, 12
Todd, Richard, 11, 12
Tomlinson, LaDainian, 13, 14, 15, 21, 22, 34
Tripucka, Frank, 12
Tucker, Justin, 23
Tuggle, Jessie, 27
Tunnell, Emlen, 25
Turner, Cecil, 31
Tyler, Wendell, 43

Umenyiora, Osi, 27
Unitas, Johnny, 12, 42, 56
Upchurch, Rick, 30, 31
Uram, Andy, 15

Van Brocklin, Norm, 9, 52, 56, 59
Van Buren, Steve, 53
Vereen, Shane, 44
Vinatieri, Adam, 20, 23, 32, 53, 55

Ware, DeMarcus, 28, 29
Warner, Kurt, 7, 41, 42
Washington, Leon, 31
Washington Redskins, 11, 12, 14, 15, 21, 22, 25, 26, 27, 28, 30, 33, 34, 35, 36, 37, 38, 39, 41, 42, 43, 44, 46, 47, 48, 49, 50, 53, 54, 55, 59, 61
Watters, Ricky, 53
Watt, J.J., 29
Wayne, Reggie, 16, 17, 54
Welker, Wes, 16, 17, 18, 44
White, James, 40, 44, 47, 54
White, Reggie, 28, 29, 45
Wilkins, Jeff, 21, 23
Williams, Aeneas, 26, 27, 55
Williams, Doug, 41, 42
Williams, Travis, 31
Wilson, Russell, 5
Winslow, Kellen, 19, 54
Witten, Jason, 16, 17
Woodley, David, 42
Woodson, Charles, 22, 25, 26
Woodson, Rod, 22, 25, 26

Young, Steve, 41, 51, 52

Zuerlein, Greg, 21, 23, 24